LIBRARY MANUAL FOR MISSIONARIES

Prepared by members

of

CHRISTIAN LIBRARIANS' FELLOWSHIP

Edited by

Clara Ruth Stone

Christian Librarians' Fellowship
1979

© 1979
Christian Librarian's Fellowship, Inc.

Printed in U.S.A.

Miller Printing Co.
Springfield, Ohio

ACKNOWLEDGMENTS:

Dewey Decimal Classification summaries in Chapter 7 reproduced from *Abridged Dewey Decimal Classification* Edition 10 (1971), by permission of Forest Press Division, Lake Placid Education Foundation, owner of copyright.

Filing rules in Chapter 9 reprinted by permission of the American Library Association from *ALA Rules for Filing Catalog Cards*, copyright © 1968 by the American Library Association.

"Criteria for selection of non-book materials," pp. 76-79 reprinted from *Developing Multi-Media Libraries* by Warren B. Hicks and Alma M. Tillin by permission of R.R. Bowker Company (A Xerox Education Company). Copyright © 1970 by Xerox Corporation.

CONTENTS

PREFACE iii

CHAPTER
1 Introduction 1
2 Administration 3
3 Services to Users of The Library 9
4 Selection of Library Materials 15
5 Acquisitions 19
6 Cataloging 26
7 Classification 39
8 Preparation of Books and Cards 47
9 Filing in The Card Catalog 61
10 Nonbook Materials 76
11 Care and Preservation of Library Materials 103
12 Planning A Library Building 107

APPENDICES
I   Definitions 111
II Reference Books 119
III Bibliography 126
IV Publishers 130
V   Library Suppliers 132
VI A Book Selection Policy 133

INDEX 135

PREFACE

Requests for help in organizing and managing a library have come to many members of the Christian Librarians' Fellowship from missionaries who, with no library science degree or previous library experience, have found themselves faced with the need to provide libraries to support their educational programs among national Christians. In responding to these requests, members soon realized the need for a library manual written especially for library staff members with little or no library training who are organizing and establishing libraries in Bible colleges, Bible schools, and seminaries that have as their primary goal the preparation of nationals for Christian ministries.

The need for such a handbook was brought to the attention of the entire membership by Ivy Olson of Wheaton College in her article, "Retrospect & Prospect," published in the December, 1969 issue of the official organ of the Fellowship, *The Christian Librarian*. Later, in the February, 1971 issue of the same periodical, the organization was challenged by three articles: "An American Librarian in the Philippines," by Dorothy K. Spidell, who had volunteered her services as a library consultant to Ebenezer Bible College in Zamboanga, Philippines; "Missions and the Christian Librarians' Fellowship," and "Proposal for the Christian Librarians' Fellowship and Libraries on the Mission Field", both by P. Paul Snezek of Wheaton College.

These challenges, along with the deepening concern and burden of the CLF membership at large, prompted the Board of Directors (meeting June, 1971 for the fifteenth annual conference at Grace College and Grace Theological Seminary, Winona Lake, Indiana) to appoint a committee to study ways in which the organization could help libraries on the mission field.

Two years later, Victoria Weah of Monrovia, Liberia, addressed CLF members at the seventeenth annual conference held at Asbury College and Seminary, Wilmore, Kentucky. Victoria, a part-time, non-professional staff member at Cedarville College Library in Ohio, expected to be called upon to help organize and administer a library in Monrovia where her husband, upon his graduation from Cedarville College, would serve as national pastor and director of a Christian day school. Her remarks again emphasized the need for a simplified but detailed guidebook for non-professionals who must stand in the gap until a professional librarian is engaged.

Under the leadership of Alberta L. Chaffe of Cedarville College, a major part of the 1973 conference program was devoted to workshop sessions for the development of topics to be included in the proposed manual. Prior to the conference, a questionnaire returned by CLF members supported the project, an outline was prepared and distributed, volunteers responded, topics and group leaders were assigned, and some writing was begun. By the close of the conference, the material, uneven and incomplete though it was, represented a significant beginning which was followed later by additional composition and editorial work by committee members.

The Editorial Committee appointed at the 1974 conference, meeting at Dallas Theological Seminary, consisted of Dr. Lucy Maddox (Spring Arbor College) and Ivy Olson (Wheaton College), with Susan Schultz (Asbury Theological Seminary) serving as chairman. When the annual conference was held at St. Paul Bible College the following year, Susan Schultz and Dr. Maddox asked to be replaced because of additional responsibilities on their own campuses. Having recently retired as librarian of Northeastern Bible College, I volunteered to serve as chairman, and Marie Loizeaux of Loizeaux Brothers, Inc. and Alberta L. Chaffe were added to the committee.

The manuscript was available for the perusal and criticism of CLF members at their twenty-first annual conference, June, 1977, at Covenant College, Lookout Mountain, Tennessee. At my request, the chairmanship was passed at that time to Mrs. Chaffe.

A significant amount of help has been received from several CLF members with experience in libraries outside of Canada or the continental United States. Among these are Lois Luesing of Bethel College, who read the manuscript, and three others who accepted the responsibility for preparing material for certain sections: Dorotha Williams (Circleville Bible College), Dorothy Spidell (Saddleback College), and Edith Taff (Southeastern Bible College).

Miss Lynn Randall, librarian of Northeastern Bible College, has been of great assistance by giving counsel, lending books, and permitting me to use the library of Northeastern Bible College.

Those who have prepared material for this manual have found of inestimable value *A Theological Library Manual* by Jannette E. Newhall, published by The Theological Education Fund, London, 1970 (available to theological schools in the Third World without cost. Others may obtain it for £2.10.)

I appreciate the patient, efficient assistance of Mrs. Helen Wang, secretary to Mr. James Kallam, Academic Dean of Northeastern Bible College, who typed and retyped the manuscript many times.

Without the understanding and encouraging support of my husband, David G. Stone, I could not have completed the manual. His assistance in proofreading and photocopying the manuscript was paramount to the project.

Clara Ruth Stone
1977

1. INTRODUCTION

You have been appointed to serve in a Bible school, Bible college or seminary library on the mission field. Perhaps others before you have established it, or you may be asked to develop a new library. This is an awesome responsibility, but it is also an exciting challenge.

We who have prepared this manual to assist you in your new position are aware of your need of the resources which God has for you. Paul in 1 Corinthians 1:30 speaks of Christ being made unto us wisdom. James 1:5 exhorts, "If any of you lack wisdom, let him ask of God, who giveth ... liberally ... and it shall be given him." With this assurance you can approach your task confidently.

The word "library" is derived from the Latin word "liber" which means "book". The first libraries were storehouses for books which only the wealthy or educated were permitted to use. The library of today, however, is much more than a building filled with books for the privileged few. It is a center where information in many forms may be obtained by anyone who seeks it. Many different terms are used to replace the word "library", such as "educational media center", "instructional materials center", "learning center", or "resource center". The librarian, therefore, is more than a "book keeper", for the functions and tasks of a librarian are varied.

In order to obtain an overview of the duties of a librarian, read this manual through without attempting to absorb the details. Return to it later for detailed instructions for each job. Do not feel, however, that you must accept all of the details given in this manual. Adapt the suggestions to fit your library situation.

Before you begin the job of organizing a new library or reorganizing one which is already established, ask for a *library committee* to work with you in an advisory capacity to evaluate your library and determine your plan of action. Find out as much as possible about the library and the school. Some important questions which should be answered are as follows:

1. How large is the school? How many students? How many teachers? What is the expected growth in numbers?
2. How large is the library staff? What are their duties? How many hours a week does each person work?
3. Where is the library housed? Is there a separate building, one room, or part of a room? How many shelves for books? How many seats for readers? What are the prospects for future expansion?
4. How many books are in the library? How many periodicals are received? How much audio-visual material and equipment?
5. How many volumes are added each year? Where and how often are books purchased?
6. What is the annual budget for the library? How much for salaries, books, periodicals, supplies, equipment?

7. How is the library organized? Are the books classified? By what system? Is there a card catalog? What type of circulation system is used?
8. How much use do students make of the library? Do teachers give library assignments? Is there a library orientation program for new students? How many books may a student take out and how long may they be kept? Is a fine charged for overdue books?
9. Are other libraries nearby which may be used by students and faculty? Is there a library which would be helpful to the library staff?
10. Are there library associations or organizations in the country? Do you participate in them?

After you have written a report evaluating the library using these questions as a guide, a discussion should be held with the faculty and administrators of the school in order to hear suggestions of services needed by faculty and students.

You will then be able to set up a program for the development of the library to become a center of service to the school and an essential member of the school program in order to give the students an adequate education. The library should provide the inspiration for students to form lasting habits of reading and study.

2. ADMINISTRATION

DEFINITIONS AND PRINCIPLES
What Is Administration?
Administration is the responsibility to manage, lead, supervise, control. This is accomplished through organization of personnel and resources. An organization is defined as the uniting of two or more persons to achieve a common goal. The organization of resources in a library is a plan for systematic arrangement of all items in the library so that any item can be readily found; that is, there is a place for each item, each item has an appropriate label assigning it to its place, and there is provision for keeping a record if that item is removed from its place for use by a patron. The techniques of organizing resources are discussed in later chapters in this manual.

What Are Some Basic Principles of Administration?
A careful analysis of problems in institutions often reveals that they could have been avoided wholly or in part by the application of good principles of administration. The following are a few suggestions:
1. **Provide for unity of management.** This means that there must be a clear understanding as to who is in charge. Ideally, this is one person. Even in work assigned to a committee, someone must be appointed as leader. When two or more persons are given equal responsibility in a given area there is a danger that neither one will proceed with the work, or there is a conflict because both are trying to do the same thing. This does not mean that the one in charge is a dictator, however. A wise administrator involves staff members in the administrative process.
2. **Manage by objectives.** To operate a library without objectives (or goals) is like building a house without a plan. The general purpose of the library is to help fulfill the purpose of its parent institution. That is the reason for its existence. However, more specific objectives must be defined. One suggestion is to list these under two major headings: resources and services. The most obvious aim under resources is to provide materials for all the courses listed in the curriculum. (To make this a performance objective it can be specifically stated that bibliographies provided for each course by the faculty will be used to fulfill this goal.) Under services, circulation services are normally the beginning with others following as staff and facilities are provided; such as reference, instruction in the use of the library, research assistance, bibliographic services, etc. The preparation of a written statement of objectives should be the joint effort of the library staff with help from faculty, administration, and students. Alumni might also give some help. Regularly the objectives should be reviewed and their implementation evaluated. A library and its services will develop in an orderly manner if its objectives are clearly stated and fulfilled.

3. **Delegate responsibility with adequate authority to carry out that task.** As soon as a library requires more than one staff member, careful thought must be given to assigning certain duties to others, expecting that those duties will be carried out to completion. These staff members must understand clearly how far their authority extends lest they become "officious" by taking authority not intended. Likewise, once the duties have been assigned, the administrator must not interfere with the staff members' work except for the supervision needed to see that the work is done satisfactorily.
4. **Establish lines of communication.** Open channels for the flow of information to and from the administrator are important. All staff members must be informed regularly about decisions and policies affecting their work. Likewise, the administrator must encourage staff members to provide information which will make for wise policy decisions. This can be accomplished through staff meetings, individual conferences, reports, memos. A general atmosphere of mutual interest and concern is important.

There are other principles, but these are a few basic suggestions. They should apply in the library and also in the institution of which it is a part. The library has a dual role: it is an administrative unit and it is an academic unit. The librarian should be involved, at least in an "ex officio" capacity, in the institution's administrative process which deals with financial planning (the budget), scheduling calendar of events, etc., so that the library will function in harmony with the total program of the institution. As part of the academic structure, the librarian must know as early as possible about new courses or degree programs planned in order to develop the resources to support them.

An Administrative Chart

A good administrative organization can best be described by a chart showing lines of responsibility and relationship within the staff. A suggested chart follows:

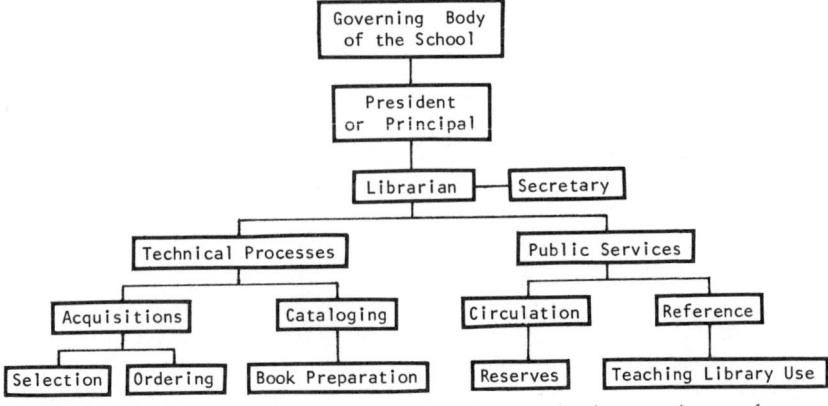

```
              Governing Body
              of the School
                    |
              President
              or Principal
                    |
              Librarian ——— Secretary
                    |
        ┌───────────┴───────────┐
   Technical Processes      Public Services
        |                        |
   ┌────┴────┐              ┌────┴────┐
Acquisitions Cataloging  Circulation Reference
   |           |             |           |
Selection  Book Preparation Reserves  Teaching Library Use
Ordering
```

This chart very simply outlines the duties which must be performed in any library, large or small. It also provides a clear understanding of what the tasks are and how they relate to each other. In a given library, staff members' names should be shown with the duties assigned to them. In a small library one or two persons must perform all the tasks shown.

THE FUNCTIONS OF ADMINISTRATION

It is difficult to describe the administrator's task, for it is a complex one, especially as the library grows. Roughly the responsibilities can be grouped under the headings: personnel, record keeping and reporting, finance, public services, physical facilities (building, furniture and equipment), and public relations. In some geographical areas, there is increasing emphasis also on cooperation with other libraries and on contributions to the library profession.

Personnel
Selection. Personnel is the key to a successful library operation. By their attitude and dedication to service, the library staff members can encourage patrons to use the library and to do so with increasing effectiveness. Therefore the staff must be selected with care on the basis of personal qualifications (for example, friendliness, sincerity, thoroughness, cooperative spirit, flexibility), educational background, and possibly previous work experience. Good health, mental, spiritual and physical, is important. Accuracy in detail needs to be stressed. (A call number incorrectly given on the spine of a book or on the catalog card may cause great time loss and inconvenience to both staff and patron. A misspelled word may cause a filing complication and result in inefficiencies which may not come to light for years!)
Training. Once the person has been chosen and the task assigned, he/she must be trained. Time taken for careful training pays dividends in self-confidence and the ability to achieve. A job description, in writing, is vital. Each person should be provided with a notebook, preferably loose-leaf, in which each assigned task is outlined as to purpose and procedure. Challenge the individual to improve the procedures and revise them accordingly (the reason for a loose-leaf notebook). Frequent review of these procedures instead of guessing or depending on a faulty memory, can avoid much trouble.
Growth and development. If the staff members are the key to the successful operation of the library, they must be provided with opportunities to grow intellectually and spiritually. They must be made to feel that they are important as persons, and thus motivated to develop their gifts in order to better serve God and fellowmen. They should be encouraged to learn the contents of books while also learning to know the library users with the aim of getting the right book to the right person at the right time. Professional reading and attendance at meetings where they may share with other library workers should be encouraged, if at all possible.
Personnel policies. Policies affecting staff working conditions should be in harmony with the overall staff policies in the institution; e.g., work-

ing hours, dress regulations (if needed), sick leave, vacation, rest periods (e.g., the midmorning or midafternoon period). These policies should be clearly stated in writing and applied with all fairness to all staff members.

Team spirit. Many libraries begin with one staff member, but as they grow, more persons are needed. No effort should be spared to develop a team spirit in the group. There must be a willingness to cooperate, to help each other to develop the best library possible. Errors discovered must be corrected without fail, for one error not corrected can lead to others and cause many complications. This requires a spirit of Christian concern and caring for one another. No one sits in judgment on another, for "To err is human". The person who made the error must not be sensitive or allow a feeling of paranoia to develop. Each error discovered and corrected in the right spirit should become a learning experience. A good sense of humor is an invaluable asset.

Record Keeping and Reporting

Records. Every library must develop its set of records to serve its own needs. If reports are required by an accrediting or government agency, records must also be kept to meet those requirements. Sometimes there is a tendency to keep too many records; so a few words of caution may be needed: 1) Keep a record if you have a purpose for that record; e.g., the number of books circulated in a given period, or sometimes at a certain time of the day or week tells how heavy the workload and how much staff is required to give adequate service. Financial records provide a basis for planning future budgets. 2) Avoid duplicate records. Check to see if this information is available in some other record already being kept. 3) Once a record has been established provide for keeping it up-to-date regularly. 4) Review the records for needed revision (additions and/or deletions).

Reports. The librarian's annual report on the activities and development of the library is perhaps the most significant reporting responsibility. Usually it is addressed to the President and the Board of Trustees (Board of Governors, or other). It is well, if possible, to develop a format under headings adequate to cover the year's work, and for ease in execution as well as review by the reader, follow that plan each year; e.g., personnel, resources, services, facilities, etc. Included in the report should be all special events or innovations which form a part of the history of that library and should be made a matter of record for future reference. A statistical summary appended to the report should show the growth of the resources, financial statistics and circulation records. These summaries, maintained year by year serve to show trends in the development of the library.

Budget Planning and Control

Normally, the money needed to operate a library is appropriated from the general budget of the school. Sometimes in a small struggling school it may not be done that way at first. It may be that any bills incurred for the library are simply turned over to the business office for payment. If this is the case, plans should be made to move toward the preparation and control of a budget especially for the library. A budget is based on need. Careful planning must be done to determine what comprises those needs, for example, books, periodicals, audio-visuals (or nonbook media), supplies, salaries, binding, equipment purchase and maintenance. In American academic libraries it is generally accepted as a norm that about 10% of the institutional budget for educational purposes (excluding buildings and development) should be used for the library. Of the budget of the library well over half, perhaps 60% is used for salaries, perhaps 30% for books, periodicals, media, and the rest for supplies, etc. These percentages would vary according to the economic situation in various countries. It is important, however, that certain sums be specified to insure that the resources of the library grow regularly and that the needed services are provided to utilize those resources as much as possible.

Record keeping in regard to library expenditures is essential. "Be not slothful in business." Every invoice must be carefully checked (to make sure it represents what was received), recorded, then signed and sent to the business office for payment. Each item in the budget should be assigned an account number which should be written on the invoice, so that the various items in the budget will be controlled, not overspent. On the basis of records kept, the new budget is prepared and adjustments are made as needed in the light of experience.

The following is an example of a budget with itemized categories and account numbers assigned:

Library Budget

Account #21	Salaries		
#23	Books, Periodicals		23 Books
		or	24 Periodicals
			25 Media
#27	Binding		
#28	Supplies		
#29	Equipment purchase		
	#29.1 Equipment maintenance (clean and repair typewriter, etc.)		

A monthly summary of invoices submitted for payment enables the librarian to chart the expenditures and prevent overspending in any area.

Services to Faculty and Students

These include first of all, circulation of library materials and reference services.

It is normal for a beginning library to use most of its money and staff time in developing the library collection and providing only the most basic services, such as circulation, reserve books, and the most basic reference service.

However, it becomes more difficult to use a library as it grows because of its technical nature. Therefore, as soon as possible greater emphasis must be placed on services to students and staff, such as more time and better qualified staff for reference service, teaching the use of the library in orientation sessions for new students, lectures to classes at the time term papers are assigned, notifying faculty of books purchased and of periodical articles which they might not see, preparation of bibliographies at faculty request, etc.

The recognition of the teaching function of the library is essential to utilizing it to the fullest. Its services and resources should be closely related to all that happens in the classroom. The library staff seeks to serve the students and teachers in every way possible to equip them for a good learning experience. The aim should be not only to provide them with the necessary resources, but also to teach them how to find the resources and to develop a method in library use which they can apply in other libraries during their lifetime ministries.

Physical Facilities

Often the library is simply assigned a room or rooms in a larger building used for administration and classrooms.

If there is a choice of rooms, several considerations should be kept in mind. Choose a location which is easily accessible, if possible in the direct flow of traffic to give it visibility.

It should be attractive and have a friendly atmosphere in keeping with the culture and climate of the geographic location. Furniture arrangement, paint on walls and equipment, plants, and draperies can all be used to produce this effect.

It should be expandable. Libraries have a way of running out of space. If an adjacent room or rooms can be designated for future use, expansion can take place with a minimum of upheaval.

It must provide adequate space for staff work areas as well as for services to the public.

The library building is discussed in chapter twelve of this manual.

Public Relations

A concern for the image that the library projects to the public (on campus as well as elsewhere) should pervade all administrative procedure. The services that are given, the manner in which they are given, the procedure for dealing with gifts to the library, the annual report and its distribution, correspondence dealing with requests for help, meeting visitors, all these are part of the public relations side of library work. They can be used to create good will toward the library or they can turn people away. Often it is not so much what is done but how it is done that matters most. The public is there and relations with that public exist for good or for ill. There is no reason for not making these relations a great asset for the library.

3. SERVICES TO THE USERS OF THE LIBRARY

The main purpose of every library is its service to its users or patrons, as they are called. The functions of cataloging, classification, and the details of processing materials are to let the patron know what is in the library, where it can be found, and how it may be borrowed from the library.

REFERENCE SERVICES

Since a library collection should be as helpful as possible to its users, someone should be available to help the patrons find the information they need. Sometimes it will mean providing answers to questions for specific information. Other times it will involve giving aid in research, providing bibliographies or locating hard-to-find materials. It may also mean teaching the use of the library so that the user can find information for himself. The sections on "Library Instruction" and "Orientation" discuss teaching the use of the library.

Every library needs books that can be consulted for specific information such as facts, statistics, and terms. These books are known as reference books — books that are referred to, not read straight through or in their entirety. Because this information can be read quickly and should always be available when needed, these reference books do not usually circulate. They should be marked with an "R" or "REF" above the call number on the spine and be given a special location in the library known as the reference section.

In general, reference books fall into two categories:
1. Those treating many subjects, such as encyclopedias, almanacs, and yearbooks.
2. Other types dealing with specific subjects such as an encyclopedia of religion, a dictionary of theology, an encyclopedia of music and musicians.

Some of the useful types of reference books that should be found in every library are listed below. Recommended titles of reference books may be found in Appendix.(2)
1. ENCYCLOPEDIAS A good, standard, accurate encyclopedia which is not the latest edition is better than a new set of uncertain reliability. The reliable set can be kept up-to-date by means of yearbooks or supplements.
2. DICTIONARIES If the main language is English, a good unabridged dictionary will not only give definitions, origins and word use, but also abbreviations and illustrative quotations. Dictionaries of the main languages of the country should be available.
3. ATLASES AND MAPS are important and should be kept up-to-date.
4. HANDBOOKS AND ALMANACS such as the WORLD ALMANAC contain many miscellaneous facts and current statistics.

5. BIOGRAPHICAL WORKS such as WHO'S WHO give information about people.
6. Specific reference books in the fields of art, music, science, literature, and Bible are important additions for reference collections.
7. INDEXES TO PERIODICAL ARTICLES are necessary for locating information in periodicals.
8. Many other types of books such as DIRECTORIES, HISTORIES, ANNUALS and BIBLIOGRAPHIES are useful in finding specific kinds of information.

Library Instruction
Every librarian gives a certain amount of instruction in the use of the library when pointing out the uses of the card catalog or when leading a patron to specific reference works. In a school, a necessary part of every student's education is instruction in the use of the library. It will help to make him more independent in his work; it will develop confidence and ability in locating information; it will save much time if he can quickly find material on a given subject through the use of the card catalog or a periodical index. It will acquaint him with tools for learning in a lifelong learning process.
Orientation. New students should be given a library tour, pointing out the location of the card catalog, reference books, reserve books, periodicals and periodical indexes, and special files such as a pamphlet file or picture file. They should be given information about library hours, borrowing privileges, length of the loan period, library fines, rules about noncirculating materials and restricted use of reserve books. This information may be included in a library handbook which is given to each new student.
Instruction in the use of the card catalog should also be given to new students. This instruction would include:
1. The different kinds of cards — author, title, and subject — and how to tell the differences in them;
2. The information given on a catalog card, such as author, title, publisher, date, and call number;
3. Subject headings and cross references such as "See" and "See also";
4. The Dewey Decimal Classification system or other system used and the parts of a call number;
5. Any special symbols such as "R" or "REF" for reference books which indicate a separate location;
6. The way in which cards are filed, especially Bible entries, and the omission of articles, "a, an, the";
7. The use of the subject catalog, using subjects in which the students are interested.

Frequently when the new student is given much information about the library at the beginning of the year in an orientation period or class, he is not able to comprehend all of it. Later in the year, when he must use the library for his classes, he realizes his need to know how to use the library correctly. At this time more specific instruction may be given in a literature class or the instruction may be a separate required course. Individual instruction is a continual task of the librarian as students ask for help.

Some teachers prefer to give library instruction in connection with a course, but often the librarian is more familiar than the teacher with the arrangement of materials and the details of the library.

Several class periods should be spent in detailed library instruction, using examples from the courses which the students are taking. Reference books should be discussed with an explanation of how to use them and the subjects or areas which various books cover. The use of periodical indexes should be carefully explained, pointing out that they are a source of more recent information than can usually be found in books. The classification system and the filing system should be explained in more detail than was done in the orientation period.

CIRCULATION SERVICES

Circulation is lending materials. Circulation procedures should be as simple as possible and should fit local needs. Unnecessary rules and restrictions should be avoided so that the best service possible may be given. Records must be kept so that if a book is not in its proper place by call number on the shelf, the book card at the circulation desk will indicate if it is checked out, when it is due back, or if it is in a temporary location such as in a display case, being mended, or on "reserve" for a class assignment.

Circulation Procedure

In processing books, a book card used for circulation should be made for each book and placed in a book pocket which is pasted inside the front or back cover. Opposite or above the book pocket is pasted the date due slip. Some book pockets can be purchased which are prepasted and have a date due slip on the pocket. Both the card and the pocket should have the call number, the accession number, and the author and the title so that they can be easily matched in checking in and out. Substitutes for purchased book pockets and cards are described in detail and examples given in chapter eight on book preparation.

When the book is checked out, the procedure is as follows:
1. The book card is taken from the book pocket.
2. The borrower signs the card and returns it to the librarian.
3. The librarian stamps the date due on the book card and on the date due slip in the book. (The library should purchase a small date due stamp which can be changed to the correct date day by day.)
4. The book card is placed in a box or charging tray with other cards from books which have been checked out the same day.

When the book is returned, the procedure is as follows:
1. The due date on the due date slip in the book is noted.
2. If the book is returned late a charge is made.
3. The librarian pulls out the book card from the circulation tray.

4. The book card is placed back in the book pocket. Be sure they match by carefully checking the call number and the accession number.
5. The book is placed on a temporary shelf or on a book truck from where it will be placed in its proper position on the library shelf.

If there is a need to renew the book, that is, lend it to the same borrower immediately, the following procedure should be noted:
1. Pull the book card from the circulation file. Make sure there is no other request for the book.
2. Restamp the book card and the date due slip in the book.
3. Put the book card with the day's circulation, for it is considered another loan.

Reserve books. A reserve book is one that is set aside for limited use for a class assignment. It is usually circulated for two hour periods and/or overnight use only. When a book is removed from the regular shelves and placed on a "reserve" shelf, the following procedure is necessary:
1. The book card is removed from the book and marked "On reserve".
2. This book card is filed at the circulation desk behind a guide card marked "BOOKS ON RESERVE".
3. A second book card, preferably of another color, is made and placed in the "reserve" book.
4. The date due slip is marked "On reserve" to identify the reserve book.
5. When the reserve book is checked out, the card is placed in a special file until it is returned. Larger fines are charged for reserved books when they are kept overdue.
6. When the book is removed from the reserve, the book card is pulled from the circulation file; the "On reserve" on the date due slip is crossed out, and the colored reserve card is destroyed.

Statistics and Records

The circulation file at the desk serves as a record for the book when it is not in its proper place on the shelves. Many libraries prefer to file the book cards by call numbers; others file by author or title. In order to know when books are overdue, the easiest method is to file all cards by the date due. A guide card should be made for each date books are due. All book cards for books due on the same date should be arranged by call number so that the book card may be found quickly when a book is returned.

	000	100	200	300	400	500	600	700	800	900	920	Pamphlets
Date												
Date												
Date												

The library should keep a record of the daily circulation in order to present an accurate record of the use of the library in the monthly and annual reports. A circulation book may be purchased from a library supply house, but a notebook with columns drawn for dates and Dewey Decimal numbers will serve well. The preceding will illustrate a page for recording statistics. This should be recorded each morning before the previous day's cards are interfiled in the charging trays.

Rules and Regulations

Certain rules and regulations for borrowing books should be made in order to be fair to all. These rules should be flexible enough to allow for exceptions and yet consistent enough so that patrons will feel the rules are fair. When the rules have been decided upon, they should be posted in the library and written in the handbook when one is prepared. The following questions should be decided in making the rules:
1. **Who will be permitted to use the library?** Some form of identification should be adopted. In a school, the school directory may be used. For outsiders, the address should be added when a book card is signed for a book. If the community is allowed to use the library, a card file of names and addresses should be kept at the circulation desk, preferably with the patron's signature. The name should be printed or typed also so the signatures on the book cards can be read.
2. **How many books can be borrowed by a patron at one time?** The size of the book collection will determine this.
3. **How long will the loan period be?** Many libraries allow two to three weeks. If the book collection is limited, it may be well to have a shorter loan period.
4. **May books be reserved?** If a book is out, patrons should have the privilege of requesting its use when returned. A note attached to the book card may have the patron's name on it.
5. **What fines will be placed on overdue books?** Many libraries place fines of 2¢ to 5¢ a day for books that are kept overdue.
6. **Will a charge be made for lost books?** Most libraries charge for the cost of replacing and processing the book.

Notices of overdue books and of fines should be sent regularly. The following forms can be used:

OVERDUE NOTICE

LIBRARY

Name
_____

Author and Title   Call Number

is overdue on _____
                        Date

Please check at the library if you have any questions.

13

FINE NOTICE

Name _____

The book _____ was returned late. The fine is_____.

4. SELECTION OF LIBRARY MATERIALS

"Selection" involves making intelligent choices of books and other materials to add to the library collection. Carefully chosen books are essential to the success of any library.

SELECTION PROBLEMS

There are many problems which complicate book selection:
1. It is estimated that there are over one million book titles in the English language available for purchase at any time. The librarian needs to learn what is available and where to secure what is selected.
2. No library budget can provide all the books which could be used. Few libraries have enough funds, but a new library feels the problem more keenly. Decisions must be made so that the most essential books are purchased first. Also, the available funds must be divided for the purchase of books in each subject area which is considered important.
3. The cost of providing shelf space for books places limits on selection. It is important that worthless books not be allowed to take up valuable shelf space. This means that the librarian needs some guidelines for judging books. Sometimes, gift books do not contribute to the library's needs and should not be put on the shelves.

SELECTION PARTICIPATION

The question of who will select materials is an important one. A primary goal of a school library is to provide resources to support the curriculum. The teachers, therefore, should be in the best position to know what the students will need. Sometimes, however, the teachers need encouragement from the librarian to recommend books so that a proper balance may be maintained.

The librarian should try to establish a good working relationship with his associates. If the library is a pleasant place to visit and if the librarian has a reputation for being helpful rather than strict, the faculty will usually cooperate. Teachers should be made aware of the bibliographies, book reviews, or catalogs available. It is the librarian's responsibility to write to publishers for catalogs, and to call teachers' attention to book reviews or bibliographies in periodicals or other sources.

A list of books that have been added to the collection should be given regularly to faculty members so they will not request the same titles for purchase, and also that they may recommend these new books to their students.

The librarian should have the authority to select other materials that are needed, including reference books. Many valuable books may be overlooked by the teachers. Some areas of the collection will be neglected unless the librarian works at keeping the materials well balanced.

The librarian is in a position to be aware of deficiencies in the collection when students' needs cannot be supplied from the books in the library. Books and other materials should be selected for those areas where the need is greater or the books are fewer. For example, the year that a new course in church music or other subject is added, special efforts should be made to purchase books in that field.

It is also important to use local resources as much as possible. These might include national libraries, local bookstores, or perhaps other schools.

SELECTION POLICY

It is advisable to have a written selection policy in order to be consistent in selecting books, periodicals and other materials for the library. This policy could be written by the librarian, or with a library committee of interested teachers. The policy should be prepared carefully, but should also be reviewed frequently.

When the policy is approved by the highest authority, whether it is the library committee, the faculty committee or the head of the school, the librarian can feel more secure, for such a policy will serve as a standard for the librarian who may be questioned about certain books which have or have not been purchased. When librarians change, the selection policy will provide a basis for continuity.

The following principles should be included:
1. The purpose of the library should be clearly stated. No library can be all things to all people, so the type of materials purchased will be determined by the library's purpose.
2. A concern for quality, regardless of quantity, should be stated.
3. If the budget is to be divided, either for different types of materials or among various departments, this should be made clear. This division can be changed yearly, determined by the need for materials in the various departments, the cost of materials in various subject areas, or the quantity available.
4. The persons who may be involved in selecting materials should be stated. Usually the librarian makes the final decision.
5. Standards for selecting books for purchase should be stated. The paragraph under SELECTION PROCEDURES offers guidelines.
6. There should be a statement on what types of materials will not be considered for purchase, such as many copies of textbooks, or currently popular books.
7. The policy on the acceptance of gifts should be made clear. It is wise to include a statement explaining that gifts which are considered unsuitable for adding to the library collection will be made available to other libraries through an exchange list, or made available to individuals who can use them, or sold and the proceeds used to buy books.
8. The library's policy in acknowledging gifts should be stated, noting

that a letter of acknowledgment will be sent to those who make gifts of books or other library materials, but that no money value will be placed on the materials by the library. It may be stated that it is the donor's responsibility to assign a value to his gift.

SELECTION PROCEDURES

The forms which list the information needed for purchase of books should be brief and easily understood. The librarian will need to know the author, complete title, publisher and his address, publication date, price, and any other information available. Forms for this purpose can be purchased or prepared by the library. They can be individual index cards or slips of paper cut to a consistent size.

To: Library
Please order the following:
Author:
Title:
Publisher:
Date of Publication:
Source of Information:
Signed:

It is best not to guarantee the purchase of any book simply because someone has asked for it. Some teachers are overzealous in recommending books without regard for the budget or the rest of the collection. There may be good reasons why a book request should be refused although it has been recommended for purchase.

The following standards should be considered when deciding whether to purchase a book:
1. Is the author qualified to write a book in the subject field?
2. Is the format of the book satisfactory — appearance, size, binding, paper, margins, type?
3. Is the information accurate and up-to-date?
4. Does the publisher have a reputation for quality books?
5. Has the book been given favorable reviews?
6. Does the doctrinal viewpoint agree with the school's doctrinal statement? If not, is its purchase still justifiable by curricular demands?
7. Does the library already have the same material in other books?
8. Is the price reasonable when compared with the amount of use the book will receive?
9. Does the library need more than one copy of the book?
10. Are there other books which are more urgently needed at this time?
11. Does the book contain any cultural or political viewpoints which might be objectionable?

SELECTION AIDS

There are many sources of information which could be used for selecting books and other library materials. The type of library will determine which ones are useful. Most of them are confined to books in the English language, although librarians must consider the language of the students using the library.

PUBLISHER'S CATALOGS list books which are currently available. These should be kept up-to-date in a file or on a shelf as sources for selection and ordering. Publisher's announcements give information about new and forthcoming books. It should be remembered that publishers recommend their own books and are in business to sell them. The librarian needs to be discriminating and not accept all claims at face value. Nevertheless, it is helpful to be on the publishers' mailing lists.

BOOK REVIEWS in current periodicals can be a great help in book selection. You should be aware that the editors' and reviewers' theological position modify their opinions. Several religious magazines publish an annual BOOKLIST of the most significant books of the past year.

For more critical selection, various BIBLIOGRAPHIES should be consulted. Some of these appear in periodicals which may already be in the collection. Subject bibliographies are available for purchase. Often a denomination's headquarters or schools can provide suggestions.

A WANT LIST may be made from teachers' requests and the librarian's suggestions so that purchases may be made as funds are available.

5. ACQUISITIONS

The acquisition of materials selected for purchase requires a method of organization for purchase and includes the following functions: order procedures, placing orders, receiving materials, accession records, business records, and gifts to the library.

ORGANIZATION FOR PURCHASE

A carefully organized and well-executed acquisitions program makes a good library collection. The librarian should be responsible for the library's purchasing program and should look upon this responsibility as an excellent opportunity to develop the best library collection possible.

Suggestions for materials for purchase may come from many people, including teachers, library staff, students and other readers. Book request forms, such as the one suggested in chapter four or a purchased multiple-copy order form similar to the one below, should be filled out and filed in a TO ORDER file until time for placing the order. Forms are completed with the author's family name written first (e.g. Smith, Robert) and files are maintained alphabetically by author.

Class No.	Author		L.C. Card Number		
Acc. No.	Title				Card Sets Ord'd
					L.C.
List Price	Place	Publisher	Year		L.J.
Dealer	Vols.	Series	Edition		WI.
No. of Copies	Recommended By	Date Ordered	Cost		Other
Order No.	Fund Charged	Date Received	S.B.N.		

ACQUISITION PROCEDURES

Verifying Purchase Requests

Before ordering a book, careful attention should be given to determine that the author and title are correct, and that the book is not in the library or on order. Those who request books frequently spell the author's name incorrectly or give an incomplete title. The following procedure is recommended:
1. Carefully inspect the book order form or book request form which has been submitted. Complete any missing information. If someone requested a book without filling out a form, prepare one.
2. Check the card catalog to see if the book is in the library. First check the author's name. If the book is a set with no main author, check the title. If you have the book, write the call number on the form and return it to the one who requested it.
3. Check the order file to see if the book is on order.
4. Check your record of books received but not yet cataloged.
5. Verify all information on the form. You may find the full name of the author if you have other books by him listed in your card catalog, but be sure it is the same author.
6. Check book reviews and publishers' catalogs for prices and other information. If you are near a large library, it may be possible to consult bibliographies there in order to verify difficult items.
7. If someone besides the librarian must approve book orders, submit the completed order forms to the proper person.

Placing orders

No specific instructions can be given about where to order books because local customs and import regulations vary from country to country. Book brokers, library jobbers, and local book stores may be used. Some libraries in schools sponsored by a mission board send their book orders to the home office of the mission board. The office takes care of the purchase, payment and shipping of the books. Other libraries order books through a mission sponsored book store. Select the agency or method that best fits your situation.

Books can be ordered directly from individual publishers, but this involves much correspondence and payment of many bills. It is much better to use one or two agents or book jobbers who will handle most of the orders.

In preparing a book order, the following steps should be taken after completing the previous steps of verification:
1. Arrange the book order forms alphabetically by author.
2. Type the order in the manner preferred by your agent, being certain to make a duplicate so that you have a copy for your records. The heading of the order should contain the name and address of the

agent or jobber, as well as your name and address (for proper billing) and the date of the order.
3. Give full information about author, title, publisher, publication date, edition, binding requested, number of copies desired, and price.
4. Write on your book order forms the date of the order and the agent's name.
5. File the book order forms alphabetically by author in your order file, (a 3" × 5" file drawer without a rod). Use guide cards to separate TO ORDER from ON ORDER. File order cards for other materials such as audio-visual materials alphabetically by title.
6. File the carbon copy of the purchase order under the name of the agent in your order correspondence file.

Receiving Materials

When a shipment arrives, unpack and verify the contents immediately. Shipping mistakes can then be corrected, if necessary. The following steps should be taken:
1. Open one package at a time and keep the packing slip or invoice with the books. Check off each book on the accompanying slip and on your copy of the purchase order. If something is missing, check the packing box and papers to see if it has been overlooked, or if there are further shipping instructions. If you have to report an error to the shipping company or book agency, include in your report the purchase order number and invoice number (usually given on the packing slip and invoice).
2. Locate in your order file the order form for each book in the package. Compare it with the book, noting the author, title, edition, publisher, and date of publication. Use the title page for this verification, not the book jacket.
3. Correct any errors on the order form, such as full name of author, incomplete title, etc. But, if the wrong book or wrong edition has been sent, ask the person who requested the book whether it should be returned for credit or kept.
4. If an item on the order or invoice is marked OS, this indicates that the item is out of stock. If the agent is waiting for a supply and will ship it later (called a "back order"), keep the OS book order form in your ON ORDER file. If the agent requests that you reorder at a later date (perhaps marked "Cancelled - reorder"), refile the order form in your TO ORDER file, marking on the form the date of the OS (Cancellation) and the suggested reorder date. If an item is marked OP, this indicates that it is out of print. Send the order form to the person who requested the item, suggesting that another item be selected. There are several book dealers who sell out-of-print books. It is helpful to obtain their catalogs and check them as soon as they arrive for any out-of-print books you may want. Order them immediately for their supply is often limited to one copy of a specific title.

5. Write the date of receipt and the price of the book on the order form. If you use a multiple copy order form, put the first two copies inside the front cover of the book for processing. File the third copy in a 3" × 5" file drawer marked "Process File" or "Books Received".
6. Carefully look through the book to see that the pages are in order and completely printed. The library term for this is "collating". Sometimes a defective book is received and should be reported to the book agency immediately. Some agents require that you do not return the book to the agent until he sends permission and instructions. Publishers usually replace a defective book as soon as it is returned. Be especially careful about collating expensive books like dictionaries and encyclopedias. Do not put any markings in books until you are sure that they are complete and correctly bound.
7. Stamp your ownership mark in the book, wherever you have decided to place it, on the first right-hand page following the title page or on the bottom or top edges of the book pages while the book is held closed.
8. Place the book on the work shelf or desk to be accessioned and cataloged.
9. After the book is processed, send the second copy of the order form to the person requesting it, informing him of its arrival.
10. Place the original copy of the book order form in a file for your accession records and type a "New Arrivals" list to be sent to all the faculty.
11. Write your book jobber or agent about any errors on the invoice. Request replacement for any imperfect copies or any incorrect titles which were sent.
12. After all adjustments have been made, sign and date the first copy of the invoice sent by the agent. Send the first copy of the invoice to the person responsible for paying bills. Keep a copy of the invoice for your records.
13. Deduct the amount of the invoice from the amount in your library budget.
14. File your copy of the invoice by date or by purchase order number.

Accession Number	Date	Author	Title	Publisher	Year	Cost	Remarks

Accession Book Page

Recording Accessions

Most libraries assign a number to each book added to the library. There are several methods of listing these accession numbers so that your library has a record of them.

One method for the small library is the accession book, either bound or loose-leaf, prepared with numbered lines and separate columns where information about each book is written. A page from a purchased accession book is shown above, but you could make one, preferably loose-leaf for ease in typing.

Each book acquired by the library is recorded on a separate, numbered line. The number of the line on which the book is recorded becomes the book's "accession number" and should be written in the book on the first right-hand page following the title page and inside the back cover. This number is never used again for another book, although the first book may be discarded or lost. When a book is lost or withdrawn from the library, a line should be drawn through the entire line of the accession record and an explanation with the date written; for example, "Lost, 3/5/77" or "Withdrawn, 8/12/78". If a lost book is replaced by another copy, a new accession number should be given to the replacement copy. When the book is cataloged, this accession number is recorded on the shelf-list card and on the book card.

The accession book is a record of the growth and the cost of the library collection. It may be used in determining the value of the library collection for insurance and inventory purposes. When gift books are added, an estimate of their value should be given.

Some libraries maintain an accession file consisting of a card or a slip of paper containing the author's name, title, publisher, date of publication and cost. The accession number is written in the upper left or upper right-hand corner of the card. Decide where you prefer to place the number and be consistent on all of the cards. The cards are filed in reverse succession, that is, the latest accession number is in the front of the file drawer. One of the multiple-copy book forms may be used for the accession file. When using an accession file instead of an accession book, some libraries use the dating method of assigning accession numbers. The year is recorded first, a dash, then the consecutive number for each acquisition. For example, the books accessioned in 1977 would begin with 77-1, 77-2, 77-3, etc. Books accessioned in 1978 would begin with 78-1, 78-2, 78-3, etc. By using this method of numbering, it is easy to determine how many books were accessioned in a given year. If you use the school year or a fiscal year, change the year prefix at the beginning of the school year or the fiscal year, rather than the calendar year.

A method for a larger library is to consider the shelf list as the accession record, for the accession number should be placed on each shelf-list card. The shelf list, however, is not an accession record in the order in which the books were added, but a record of materials in the order in which they appear on the shelves by classification number.

Receiving Gifts

Gifts are a valuable source of enriching the library book collection. Most libraries receive books and other library materials as gifts from individuals or groups. Send a cordial letter of appreciation promptly to the donor. Keep copies of these letters in a file of gift correspondence, arranged alphabetically by the donor's family name. This file is valuable if a donor visits the school and wishes to see how his gift was used.

Use much discretion when accepting gifts. Donors may send books which are not suitable for a school library. The library should not fill its shelves with books of outdated material or subjects that will never be used in the curriculum.

Most librarians prefer to accept only gifts which have no restrictions attached. The no-restrictions rule can avoid many difficulties which may arise should the donor impose various limitations. Donors should be told tactfully that books will be gratefully received, and after checking carefully the library will give any books not needed to another library or to students, or sell them and use the proceeds to buy needed titles.

Another problem may arise when a library is offered a large group of books (such as someone's personal library) with the restriction that the books be kept together as a special collection. Books in special collections are not used readily because they are not shelved with other books on the subject. Try to persuade donors to allow their books to be integrated with the rest of the collection. If a list of the books is kept under the donor's name in the gift correspondence file, they can be identified if necessary.

When you list gifts in the accession book, write the family name of the donor in the "Cost" column, with an estimated value for insurance purposes. If several books are received from the same donor, list them on successive lines, if possible.

Promptness and tact in acknowledging gifts can be very beneficial to the library. Many people would be glad to donate books if they knew where to send them. If your mission board is made aware of your needs and your desire for gift books, perhaps they could suggest possible donors and could secure gift books for your library.

6. CATALOGING

After a book has been received, properly recorded and accessioned, the next step is to prepare it for use. The book should be opened correctly and checked for defects before it is accessioned. In order for the library patron to be able to know what is in the library and where it can be found, an index must be prepared. This index, usually a card catalog, is a list of books, periodicals and other materials. Each entry is prepared on a standard size card, usually 7.5 × 12.5 cm. with a hole punched at center bottom through which a rod is inserted to hold the cards in place when they are filed in alphabetical order in a tray or drawer.

The functions of cataloging and classification are basic steps in preparing the card catalog. Although these two steps are closely related, they are discussed in separate chapters. Libraries all over the world follow basic rules that have been agreed upon. These are very complete so that they will meet the needs of large universities. They may be simplified for smaller libraries, but it is important that the basic rules be followed. When the library increases in size, it will not be necessary to change the cards or catalog the books again if the basic rules have been carefully followed.

Cataloging, which means the preparation of cards to describe each book, includes descriptive cataloging, subject cataloging and shelf listing. Descriptive cataloging describes the physical structure of a book by giving the author, title, publisher, date, number of pages and other facts. Subject cataloging is making cards for the main topics or subjects discussed in a book. Shelf listing is making a card for each title so that the cards may be arranged by classification number the same way books are arranged on the shelves. Classification means assigning a number symbol to a book according to the subject with which it deals.

DESCRIPTIVE CATALOGING

It is advisable to write by hand the first draft of your catalog cards, for you can easily make any corrections. An assistant may be trained to type the cards from your handwritten ones. Using a slip of paper the size of the catalog cards, write the description of the book in the prescribed form. Details for typing the cards are given in chapter eight. You should get all the information possible from the title page of the book, not from the cover or book jacket.

The author's name is written on the fourth line from the top of the card with the family name first, followed by the given or first name. If the middle name is known or can easily be found, write that also. If you know only the initial of the first or middle name, leave eight typewriter spaces after each initial so that you can fill in the name in case you learn it later. If the author's birth and death dates are known or can be easily found, they follow on the same line as his name. These dates may be omitted, but if there are two authors with the same name listed in your card catalog, it is wise to use their dates to distinguish them. Other author forms are discussed in the section at the end of this chapter under "Personal Author as Main Entry". If the person whose name is on the title page is not the author, but an editor or compiler, note this after his name by "ed." or "comp."

Write the title on the fifth line, indented two spaces like a paragraph. Capitalize only the first letter of the first word in the title and proper names. Place a period at the end of the title. If there is a sub-title, it comes immediately after the title, separated from the title by a comma, semi-colon or colon. Follow the punctuation on the title page, if possible. If the title is too long for one line, the next line should start at the first indentation, that is, even with the author's last name. If there is more than one author, a comma should follow the title, then "by" followed by the author statement. The author statement is the author's name and any joint authors. Do not give more than three names. If more than three authors are given, write only the first author and add the phrase "and others". Place a period after the author statement. After the title and author statement, write any information about the edition, for example, "rev. ed." for revised edition or "5th ed." for the fifth edition, or "2nd ed. rev. and enl." for the second edition which has been revised and enlarged.

The imprint starts two spaces after the period at the end of the title transcription, that is, either the title alone or after the title and author or edition information. The imprint includes the place of publication followed by a comma, then the copyright date or the year of publication followed by a period. If several places of publication are given, use the first mentioned place. If you cannot find the place of publication, use the abbreviation n.p. for "no place" enclosed in brackets. The place of publication is followed by its country, state or similar designation if it is necessary to identify the place or to distinguish it from another place of the same name. Use abbreviations for such designations. The name of the publisher may be shortened to one word, as Nelson, instead of Thomas Nelson. The following parts of the publisher statement are considered unnecessary: a) phrases such as "published by", "published for", and the word "publisher", b) the initial article except when necessary for clarity, c) phrases such as "and company", "and sons" and their foreign equivalents, d) terms meaning "incorporated" or "limited". The copyright date may be found on the back of the title page and should be written preceded by "c" as c1974. If the copyright date is not given, use the publication date which may be found on the title page or in the preface or at the end of the book. If you cannot find the date of the publication, use "n.d." meaning no date. When you use the copyright date given on the back of the title page, be sure to notice whether there have been later editions or revisions. The important information to be recorded is either the copyright date, the date of the latest revision, or the date of the latest edition. Reprint dates may be ignored.

On the line below the imprint, at the second indentation, write the collation, that is, the physical description of a book, giving such information as number of pages, number of volumes, illustrations. If the preface is important, you may write the paging for the preface as it is given, usually in small roman numerals, for example xvii. For the number of pages, use the last arabic numbered page. Sometimes the index is numbered separately in roman numerals, but it is not necessary to record it. The abbreviation "p." is used for pages. If the book is illustrated, write "illus." two spaces after the paging. Important maps should be indicated by "maps". If the book is part of an important series, write the name of the series enclosed in parentheses on the same line with the collation.

Information about the book such as a good bibliography or a change of title may be indicated in a note on the line below the collation, starting at the second indentation.

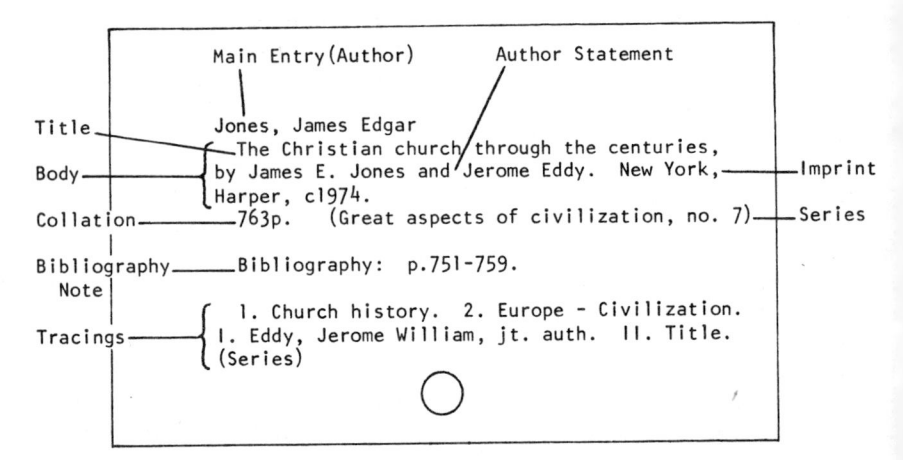

```
                    Main Entry(Author)        Author Statement

Title             Jones, James Edgar
                    The Christian church through the centuries,
Body              by James E. Jones and Jerome Eddy. New York,      Imprint
                  Harper, c1974.
Collation         763p. (Great aspects of civilization, no. 7)      Series

Bibliography      Bibliography: p.751-759.
    Note
                   1. Church history. 2. Europe - Civilization.
Tracings           I. Eddy, Jerome William, jt. auth. II. Title.
                   (Series)
```

You have now completed the description of the book, but there are many differences in books which may not fit the instructions above. Details for such differences are given in the section at the end of this chapter under THE MAIN ENTRY.

SUBJECT CATALOGING

A patron who wants a book on a specific subject may not know the name of an author who has written on that subject nor the title of a book about the subject. Book classification is an arrangement of books by subject, but most library users do not know the classification system well enough to locate a subject by the number which represents a certain subject. Also, a book has only one classification number, but it may deal with several subjects which will be important to library users. The book may be located, therefore, if the additional subjects are found in the subject catalog.

The subject catalog, which is an index to the books in the library on many subjects, is a file of cards arranged alphabetically by subject instead of by author or title. A separate subject card is made for each book in the library on a given subject. Some libraries arrange all of their author, title and subject cards in one alphabetical catalog, but many others find that users like a divided catalog, that is, one card catalog for author and title cards and another card catalog for subject cards.

In order to be consistent in preparing subject cards, you should have a prepared list of subject headings. A subject heading is a word or a group of words indicating a subject under which all material dealing with the same theme is entered in a catalog. Some librarians may prefer to make their own subject heading list, but most librarians take advantage of the experience of those who have prepared printed lists. One of the most widely used lists is *Sears List of Subject Headings* which is revised periodically and is published in several languages. The method of using Sears is fully explained in the preface and the introductory section, "Subject Headings: Principles and Applications of the Sears List" (11th ed., 1977), which gives a brief course in subject cataloging.

Use the following rules to help you decide the form of words to use for subject headings. These rules will suggest where to look up a subject in the printed list you use.

Rule 1. A single word, usually a noun, is the simplest subject heading. Words may be used in the plural to refer to classes of objects.

ANTHROPOLOGY	ANIMALS
CALVINISM	HYMNS
HEAVEN	MUSICIANS
MARRIAGE	PRAYERS

Rule 2. Words may be explained or subdivided by adding another word or phrase. Sometimes this added word precedes the noun (normal order); at times the added word follows after a comma (inverted order).

Normal Order	Inverted Order
BIBLE STORIES	AFRICA, SOUTH
CAMPUS EVANGELISM	ATHLETES, CHRISTIAN
CHILD STUDY	MISSIONS, HOME
CHRISTMAS SERMONS	STEWARDSHIP, CHRISTIAN

Rule 3. Phrases may be used when a single word will not express the subject.

BIBLE AND SCIENCE
CHRISTIANITY AND COMMUNISM
CHURCH WORK WITH ADULTS
CITIES OF REFUGE

Rule 4. A personal name may be a subject if a book or a chapter is written about the person. The name is typed in capital letters, as are all subject headings, in inverted order.

CALVIN, JOHN, 1509-1564

The personal name may also be a fictional or mythological one. The name of any institution, organization or governmental body may be used. The name of any geographical feature may be used.

Rule 5. Subjects may be subdivided in order to show the specific content of different books. Large libraries use many subdivisions, but a small library will find the general subject heading satisfactory. Most libraries may want to use subdivisions under subjects like Church history.
  CHURCH HISTORY - PRIMITIVE AND EARLY CHURCH
  CHURCH HISTORY - MIDDLE AGES
  CHURCH HISTORY - 15th CENTURY

Rule 6. Special subject headings are used for certain *kinds* of books such as dictionaries, directories, concordances, grammars, pictures, maps.
  BIBLE - CONCORDANCES
  HEBREW LANGUAGE - DICTIONARIES
  INDIA - MAPS
  LATIN - GRAMMARS

Rule 7. Cross reference cards are the connecting links in the subject catalog. There are two kinds of cross reference cards: *See* and *See also*. *See* reference means that all material on a subject is listed under a different subject heading. *See also* reference means that more material, with a different emphasis, will be found under a different heading.

CHRIST	PSALMODY
See	See also
JESUS CHRIST	CHURCH MUSIC
	HYMN TUNES
	HYMNS

Getting Started

It is recommended that you assign your subject headings at the same time you assign a classification number to a book. Since book classification is an arrangement of books by subject, the classification scheme is a guide to subjects.

In order to decide upon the classification number and the subject headings of a book, read the title page, look over the table of contents carefully, read the preface or introduction. If you have not yet been able to determine the subject, it may be necessary to skim through the text. Chapter summaries and final summaries may be helpful. If the subject is one with which you are not acquainted, you may need to look up definitions in a standard dictionary, an encyclopedia or in a subject dictionary such as a dictionary of theological terms.

When a given topic may have a number of different terms which might be used, use the term which is most familiar to your patrons, or one which most clearly describes the contents of the book.

Do not make many subject headings for each book, for it will take more of your time as well as the time of the typist and the one who files the cards. Generally, the rule would be to make only one subject heading for a book. You should seldom make more than two. However, if you do not have a large library and if you do not have entire books on a subject, you may want to make subject analytic cards, which give page numbers for parts of books, as well as a general subject heading for the whole book.

Example: *Major doctrines of the Christian faith* would have the general subject heading THEOLOGY. This would be adequate for a large library. A small library may decide to make a subject analytic card for each of the doctrines discussed: GOD, JESUS CHRIST, HOLY SPIRIT, ESCHATOLOGY, etc.

```
230       THEOLOGY
CHA       Chafer, Louis Sperry
 m           Major doctrines of the Christian faith.
          Revell, 1932.
             372p.
```

Subject card for a major part of the contents

```
230       HOLY SPIRIT, p.3-70.
CHA       Chafer, Louis Sperry
 m           Major doctrines of the Christian faith.
```

```
230       GOD, p.72-110.
CHA       Chafer, Louis Sperry
 m           Major doctrines of the Christian faith.
```

Subject analytic cards for specific part of the book

When a subject is chosen and used, pencil a check or a tick (✓) in your subject heading list to the left of the heading chosen. Indicate by a check (✓) all cross references made. If you have to supply a heading for a topic not covered, write it in the margin of the subject heading list in its alphabetical sequence, check (✓) it and write the source where you found the subject and any cross references you may make.

When you have decided on the subject headings to be used for a book, records or "tracings" of the subjects must be placed on the main entry card in order that all cards for the book can be *traced* and withdrawn from the card catalog if the book is lost or discarded from the library. The tracings are placed at the bottom of the card, at least two lines below the rest of the card. Beginning at the second indentation, number each item in sequence, with the subject headings first, using arabic numerals. All other added entries use roman numerals except the series card. The series card is the final tracing with the word "Series" in parenthesis: (Series).

Write the tracings as a paragraph, if necessary, bringing the second line out to the first indentation.

    1. Church history.   2. Europe - Civilization.
    I. Title. (Series)

Some libraries place the tracings on the back of the catalog card upside down so that the back of the card can be seen for easy reading without taking it from the catalog drawer.

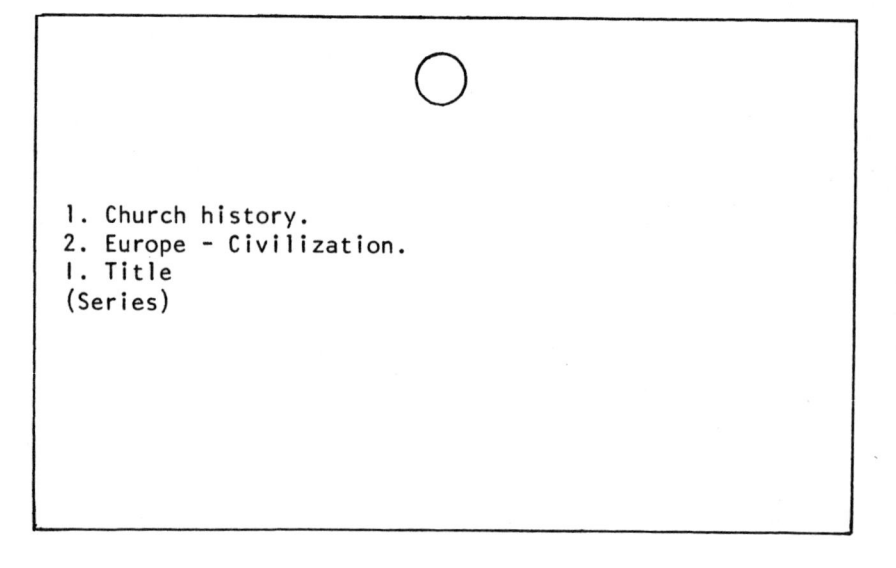

```
           ___
          (   )
           ‾‾‾




   1. Church history.
   2. Europe - Civilization.
   I. Title
   (Series)




```

SHELF LISTING

The shelf list is a file of catalog cards arranged according to classification number the same way the books are arranged on the shelves, with one card for each title (book or set of books). Within the same classification number, the cards are arranged alphabetically by author, except for biography, where the cards are arranged alphabetically by the name of the person whose life is described, the biographee. If there are two or more books about the same person, the cards are further arranged alphabetically by author. If there are two or more editions of a book, the cards are arranged chronologically, the earliest date first. If there is a separate collection, such as a reference room, the call number should have a location symbol such as "R" or "REF" and all cards for that collection should be filed separately from the main collection, in classification order. If fiction books are identified by "F" rather than being incorporated into the classification schedule, the cards are filed separately from the main collection, arranged alphabetically by author and then by title.

The shelf-list card should be a duplicate of the main entry card, but it should also show the accession number, indicate the number of copies and volumes and price at the time of acquisition. If more room for this information is needed than is available on the face of the card, flip the card and place the information on the back. Do not use inclusive lists on the shelf-list card, such as V.1-8, for you should show an accession number for each volume and each copy.

```
270
Lat      Latourette, Kenneth Scott, 1884-
 h           A history of Chritianity.  Harper, 1953.
             1516p.

             1. Church history.  I. Title.

4762  6/73  5.17
```

EXAMPLE OF SHELF-LIST CARDS

```
270.8
Vid      Vidler, Alexander Roper, 1899-
  c         The church in an age of revolution; 1789
          to the present day.  Penguin, 1962.
          374p.

               1. Church history - Modern period.  I. Title.
4669   3/65   3.22
7362   5/67   3.98

                            O
```

EXAMPLE OF SHELF-LIST CARDS

The shelf list is one of the most valuable records in the library. It is used to take inventory to see if any books are missing. It may be used as a record for insurance to determine the value of the collection. It shows how many copies of a book the library owns, as well as how many books the library has in a given classification. It may be used as a basis for a bibliography or reading list on a special subject. The cataloger uses the shelf list to determine how certain subjects have been classified and how different classification numbers have been used. When the complete call number, including a Cutter number or author number, is used, the cataloger must check the shelf list to make certain that another book does not have the same call number. The shelf list is also used to assign copy numbers.

The shelf list should be kept in file drawers convenient to the area where cataloging is done. It should not be used by students except under strict supervision, for its records are too important to risk being damaged in any way.

THE MAIN ENTRY

An **entry** is a name or word under which a card is entered or filed in the card catalog. There are author entries, title entries, subject entries, series entries, and others. The **main entry** is the basic catalog card which gives the most complete information about a book. Other cards for the book may be shortened, but the **main entry** card is the standard for all the other cards, which are known as **added entries**, because they are **additional** or secondary to the **main entry**. The added entries may include a title card, joint author card, illustrator card, series card, subject card and others. The information for the main entry is taken from the title page.

The **main entry** card is usually a personal name since most books have a person responsible for the text. In some cases an organization which is responsible for the book would be the main entry. In other cases, such as a periodical, yearbook, or anonymous book, it is difficult to assign responsibility for authorship, thus the main entry is under title.

Personal Authors As Main Entry

When one person is listed on the title page as author, the main entry is under the author's name with the family name written first, for example, *Mediterranean echoes* by James Hrdlicka would be entered as:
   Hrdlicka, James
      Mediterranean echoes.

When two or more persons are listed on the title page as authors, make the main entry under the first name which appears on the title page. Use only one name on the top or author line on the catalog card. Put the other names following the title in the title paragraph. For example, if the title page shows: *Studies in educational psychology*, by Lester G. Smith, James Addams and Louise Marshall, published by Harper in 1960, the card format is:
   Smith, Lester George
      Studies in educational psychology, by Lester G.
   Smith, James Addams and Louise Marshall. New
   York, Harper, c1960.

When the names of more than three authors are given, mention only the first author and add the phrase "and others". Example: *The sages of Windsor*, by Marcia Attles, Geoffrey Sim, Walter Barth, and Ian Worth.
   Attles, Marcia
      The sages of Windsor, by Marcia Attles
   and others. New York, Knopf, c1976.
      328p.

Editors And Compilers As Main Entry

Many books are edited or compiled by one person, but not written by him. Usually this kind of book is a collection of the writings of many different authors. If the name of the editor or compiler appears on the title page, the main entry is entered under the name of the editor or compiler, followed by a comma and "ed." or "comp." It is not necessary to write the name of the editor or compiler in the title paragraph. Examples: *Christian faith and modern theology.* Edited by Carl F.H. Henry.
    Henry, Carl F   H   ed.
        Christian faith and modern theology. Great
    Neck, N.Y., Channel, c1964.
        426p.

Evidence that demands a verdict. Compiled by Josh McDowell.
    McDowell, Josh, comp.
        Evidence that demands a verdict; historical
    evidences for the Christian faith. San Bernar-
    dino, Calif., Campus Crusade, c1972.
        387p.   illus.

If the writings of one author have been edited by another person, the main entry would be the author of the writings rather than the editor, since the author of the writings is mainly responsible for the work. The editor would be mentioned after the title in the title paragraph.
Example: *The poetry of Robert Frost.* Edited by Edward Connery Lathem.
    Frost, Robert, 1874-1963.
        The poetry of Robert Frost. Edited by
    Edward Connery Lathem. New York, Holt,
    c1969.
        xx, 607 p.

Organizations As Main Entry

Many works are sponsored by institutions, associations, churches or denominations. The main entry for such works is under the name of the organization which sponsored the work. Such an entry is called a **corporate entry**. It is important to find the official name of the organization and always use it in the same form.
Example: *Evangelism-in-depth; experimenting with a new type of evangelism, as told by team members of the Latin America Mission.*
    Latin America Mission.
        Evangelism-in-depth; experimenting with
    a new type of evangelism, as told by team
    members of the Latin America Mission.
    Chicago, Moody, c1961.
        126p.

Some organizations may join together to form a new corporate body, or may change names. In such cases cross reference cards must be made.

A cross reference card is a card which refers the user of the catalog from one term to another. There have been many changes in the names of denominations and mission boards recently. A new main entry should be made under the present name of the organization with cross references to the previous name.

    The Evangelical Alliance Mission
        For materials published prior to 1964
      See
    The Scandinavian Alliance Mission

    The Scandinavian Alliance Mission
      See also
    The Evangelical Alliance Mission

    Evangelical United Brethren Church
        For materials published before 1946
      See
    Church of the United Brethren in Christ (new constitution)
    The Evangelical Church

Title As Main Entry

Sometimes no author or editor can be found, as in an anonymous classic or in a work such as an encyclopedia, a yearbook, or a periodical where the editor changes often. The main entry for such a work is entered under the title. Begin the title at the first indentation where the name of the author is placed if you know it, and indent all later lines to the 2nd indentation. This is called a hanging indentation. For annuals and yearbooks which are published regularly, give the date of the first volume if you know it. If it is not known, use the date of the earliest volume you have. Put a hyphen after it. Do not put the number of pages in the current volume, but put "v."
Example:
    The world almanac and book of facts. New
      York World Telegram, 1868-
        v. illus., maps.

Bible Entries

The basic rule for making the main entry card for the Bible is always to use the word "Bible" followed by information about the portion of it, that is, whether it is Old Testament or New Testament or if it is a part of one of the Testaments or one book of the Bible, next the language of the translation, then the name of the translator or version, and the date of copyright or publication. If the text is a paraphrase or selections, the pro-

per subheading "Paraphrase" or "Selections" follows the language and version, followed by the date. In a small library you may omit the translator or version, but use the date.
Example:
    Bible. English. American Standard. 1901
    Bible. English. American Standard. Selections. 1939
    Bible. English. Authorized. 1910
    Bible. English. Authorized. New Scofield. 1967
    Bible. English. Berkeley. 1959
    Bible. English. Living Bible. Paraphrase. 1971
    Bible. O.T. Greek. Septuagint. 1855
    Bible. O.T. Hebrew. Harkavy. 1916
    Bible. O.T. Pentateuch. English. Tyndale. 1967
    Bible. O.T. Psalms. English. Alexander. 1850
    Bible. N.T. French. Synodal. 1922
    Bible. N.T. German. Luther. 1951
    Bible. N.T. Greek. Nestle. 1936
    Bible. N.T. Gospels. English. Moffatt. 1930
    Bible. N.T. John. French. 1956

    In order to distinguish between the different versions of the Bible, you may use "Cutter" letters to designate the version, such as "Aut" for authorized or King James Version, "Rev" for Revised Standard Version. Use a second set of Cutter letters to designate a special edition of the authorized or other versions, such as $_{Cam}^{Aut}$ for *The Cambridge Shorter Bible,* which is the authorized version. By this means, all editions of the same version will be arranged together on the bookshelves.

220.5	
Aut	Bible. English. Authorized. Selections. 1928.
Cam	The Cambridge shorter Bible. Arr. by A. Nairne, T.R. Glover, and Sir Arthur Quiller-Couch. Cambridge, University Press, c1928.
	890p.

7. CLASSIFICATION

Classification in its basic form is an arrangement according to some systematic division into classes or groups. Library classification is the arrangement of books so that those dealing with similar subjects are placed together on the shelves, making it easy for the user to find the library materials needed. Books written in a particular form, such as poetry or dictionaries, are also usually arranged together. Depending upon the classification system used, numbers or letters, or a combination of numbers and letters, are assigned to a book according to its subject.

CLASSIFICATION SYSTEMS

If a library is to be organized by subject, a system of classification should be adopted. Several classification systems have been developed, each with its own notation system. Some of the systems which are in use around the world include:
Bliss Classification, developed in the United States by Henry Bliss, used in several African libraries;
Chinese Classification, by K.C. Liu;
New Classification Scheme for Chinese Libraries, published by Taiwan National University;
Classification Decimale Universelle, published in France and used in French speaking areas, but also published in several languages, including English;
Colon Classification, developed in India by S.R. Raganathan;
Korean Decimal Classification, published by the Korean Library Association;
Nippon Decimal Classification, sponsored by the Japan Library Association;
Union Seminary Classification, developed by Miss Julia Pettee for the library of Union Theological Seminary in New York;
Classification of the Library of Tainan Theological College, Tainan, Taiwan, which is a modification of the Union Seminary Classification.
The two most widely used systems in the United States are the *Library of Congress Classification* and the *Dewey Decimal Classification*. The *Library of Congress Classification*, which was developed for a very large general library, is used in many important universities in Africa, Asia and Latin America. The *Dewey Decimal Classification* is the system most widely used in small libraries in the United States and in theological libraries outside the United States. Partial or complete translations of the *Dewey Decimal Classication* are available in many languages. Information about translations in local languages may be obtained by writing to Forest Press, Inc., Lake Placid Club, New York, 12946, USA.
Choosing the standard classification system you will use is not easy, for no system is entirely satisfactory for every situation. If your library is

already classified in a modern and regularly revised system, do not consider making a change. If it is not classified in a modern system, you may consider the system which is used in your region so that you may get help with special problems from near-by libraries or from library school courses. If your students are familiar with the local system, your using it would be an assistance to them. Another point which should be considered is whether the system you choose is available in the language of your country. If not, can the system be used readily in English or another language in which it has been translated? Do not try to devise your own system, but choose a standard system and follow it without making any local changes.

The Dewey Decimal Classification, the system most widely used in the United States (especially in small libraries) and well known internationally, is the system recommended in this manual. It was developed in 1873 by Melvil Dewey, but has been constantly revised to meet new conditions and new terminology. An abridged edition is available for use by small libraries.

USING THE DEWEY DECIMAL CLASSIFICATION SYSTEM

Dewey Decimal Classification, which uses a notation system composed of arabic numerals, arranges all knowledge as represented by books into ten broad subject classes. Each class is divided into ten divisions, each division into sections. Each division and subdivision can be divided by adding a decimal point and as many decimal digits as needed. All Dewey numbers must have at least three digits (220, 226, 268), but if more precise classification is desired, a decimal point and more digits may be added (220.13, 226.2, 268.432).

First Summary
The 10 Classes

000	Generalities
100	Philosophy and related disciplines
200	Religion
300	The social sciences
400	Language
500	Pure sciences
600	Technology (Applied sciences)
700	The arts
800	Literature and rhetoric
900	General geography, history, etc.

Second Summary
The 100 Divisions

200	Religion
210	Natural religion
220	Bible

230 Christian doctrinal theology
240 Christian moral and devotional theology
250 Christian pastoral theology
260 Christian social and ecclesiastical theology
270 History and geography of Christian church
280 Christian denominations and sects
290 Other religions and comparative religion

The next step is to divide each of the 100 divisions into ten sections. The sections for 220 Bible are as follows:

220 Bible
221 Old Testament
222 Historical books
223 Poetic books
224 Prophetic books
225 New Testament
226 Gospel and Acts
227 Epistles
228 Revelation
229 Apocrypha, pseudepigrapha, etc.

The Index to Dewey, which is listed in alphabetic subject order, is called a "Relative" Index because it shows the relationship between various aspects of a specific subject. Since the basic arrangement of Dewey is by discipline or branches of knowledge, and a given subject may appear in any number of disciplines, the Relative Index helps to show the different aspects of the subjects and their appropriate places in the classification scheme. You will find the Index very useful, but a word of caution is advisable. Do not assign to the book you are classifying the classification number given in the Index without first checking the number with the General Tables to be sure that number is correctly related to the general subject under which it falls. Check also to see if there is a subdivision which would be more specific. For example, if you are classifying a book on marriage, the Relative Index is as follows:

Marriage
  counseling see Counseling
  ethics
    philosophy   173
    religion
      Christian   241
    law   347.6
    rites
      customs   392
      etiquette   395
  sociology   301.42
  statistics   see Demography

  see also   Sex relations

The number which you will choose to classify the book, therefore, will depend upon the emphasis which the author places on marriage, whether it is ethical, religious, sociological, customs, etiquette.

GENERAL PRINCIPLES

There are several general principles which will help you decide where to classify a book.
1. Class the book first according to subject and then by literary form (fiction, drama, poetry, sermons, dictionary, etc.) in which the subject is presented, except in the general works (000) class and in literature (800) where form is most important. For example, a book of sermons on Faith would be classed in 234.2 instead of 252, which is the Dewey number for sermons.
2. Class a book where it will be most useful. This means that you will take into consideration the nature of your collection and the needs of your users. A small library may use a **broad classification**, that is, classify a book only in main classes and divisions without using long decimal class numbers; whereas a large library may use **close classification**, which means classifying each subject as completely or as fully as possible, using after the decimal point all the numbers given in the classification schedule. A large library might classify the King James Version of the Bible in 220.5203, but a small library with few Bibles may place it in 220.
3. Place a book in the most specific number that will contain it, rather than in the general topic. For example, if you have many books on the Reformation, it would be better to place them in 270.6 than in 270, which is the general number for church history. You should check the classification schedule carefully to see how the subject is subdivided. However, the inexperienced classifier is inclined to be too specific. It is wasted effort to use the most specific number for each book in a small collection and an unnecessary burden to the library user.
4. When the book deals with two or three subjects, place it with the predominant subject or with the one treated first. When the book deals with more than three subjects, place it in the general class which combines all of them. Make subject heading cards for all of the subjects which are treated equally, if you think your students may use them.
5. Classify a book primarily according to the intent of the author and the obvious purpose of the book. For example, a book on the Christian and politics would be placed in 261.7 (Christianity and civil government), not in 323.1 (Relation of state to individuals and groups).

Getting Started in Classifying

Use the Abridged Dewey Decimal Classification except for the 200 section. Read carefully the introduction to the Abridged Dewey. You may find it technical, but it will give you a good overview of how it should be used. After you have classified several books, read the introduction again. The information will then be more meaningful to you. You may find that you need to refer to the introduction many times.

In assigning a classification number to a book, you should use the procedure which you use in assigning subject headings. It is recommended that the two steps be done at the same time, for the classification number is a guide to subject headings and subjects are a guide to classification.

If you have many new books to classify, or if you want to classify your entire library, you may find your work made easier and more efficient by first grouping the books by broad subject areas. Make a sign for each general subject you have, such as: Philosophy, Psychology, Bible, Theology, Sociology, Greek, Biology, English Literature, American Literature, History, Reference Books, etc. Place the signs on tables or on empty shelves and rearrange the books under the subjects you have chosen. As you work, you may realize that you need to make other general subjects, for you may have some books which do not fit under the subjects you first selected. After you have arranged the books by broad subjects, you may want to rearrange some of the sections into more specific subjects, such as your Bible or Theology section. The summary tables in the Abridged Dewey Classification will be much help in arranging the books.

Before you assign a specific classification number or subject heading to a book, you must find out what the book is about. First, read the title page of the book, but NEVER classify by the title alone. The title may give you information about the contents of the book, but it could be vague or misleading. The synopsis of the contents which is printed on the book jacket may be of some help to you, but do not use it as the final basis for your decision, for that information was written primarily to sell the book. Some words which you may find on the book jacket which may be helpful to you are "novel", "fictional account", "biography", "historical treatment", "devotional thoughts". The preface and introduction should help you determine the author's plan or objective. The preface is usually written by the author and the introduction may be written by someone who tries to explain the author's point of view. The table of contents or chapter headings may give you valuable clues to the subject matter of the book. If you have not yet been able to determine the subject, the index may help you. Sometimes, however, you may need to skim through or read part of the text in order to make a firm decision.

Look at the Summary Tables at the front of the Dewey Classification book to find the class and division which fit the subject you have chosen, or use the Relative Index to select the class.

Turn to the main classification schedule to check whether the number you have chosen fits your book in relation to other numbers in that section.

Check your **shelf list** to find what other books you have classified in the number you have chosen. If they are similar, then use the number.

Write the classification number in pencil on your work slip (the temporary card from which your typist will type the set of cards). Determine the subject headings and write them in pencil. Place this slip in the book while you classify other books in the group. When you have classified all of the books in this group, compare the classification numbers to see if you have been consistent.

The entire number and letter symbol assigned to a book is known as the "call number". In some large libraries where patrons do not have access to the books, they must "call for" or request the book they want to use by giving the "call number" to a clerk who obtains the book. The full call number includes the subject classification number and book number which consists of a letter or letters plus a number to represent the author's name; a "work" letter to indicate the title; other designations for special location, edition, volume or copy number. **Book numbers** and **work mark** are used to distinguish one book from others on the same subject so that each title will have a distinctive **call number**. They also provide a way by which books in the same classification may be arranged on the shelves alphabetically by author and then by title.

Some libraries use a combination of letters and numbers to form the **author number** which stands for the family name of the author. This combination is known as "Cutter number" for it was developed by C.A. Cutter. It has been expanded from two to three digits by Kate Sanborn. The tables used to find the correct numbers are called the Cutter-Sanborn tables. Instead of using the tables, some libraries use only the first three letters of the author's family name. Others write the family name in full. If you decide to use only the first three letters, there may be times when you must use four or more letters if several authors have the names that begin with the same first three letters. At times you may have a book which does not have an individual author. Such books are given a book number to represent the first word in the title, excluding a, an or the.

Example of **author numbers**:

Bible Doctrine by Arthur Hailey would be classified in 230.

CUTTER	FIRST LETTERS	FULL NAME
230	230	230
H151b	Hai	Hailey
	b	b

It is possible to have two or more titles by one author which are concerned with the same subject, thus having the same classification number. A "work" letter or "mark" is added to the **Cutter name** or **author name** to distinguish between the two titles. The "work mark" is formed by using the first letter of the first word of the title excluding a, an or the.

Example of "work mark":

Major Bible themes and *Systematic theology* by Louis Sperry Chafer are classified in 230. The Cutter number for Chafer is C433. The call numbers would be:

Major Bible themes	Systematic theology
230	230
C433m	C433s

When letters or the full name are used as the author number, the work mark is placed below the letter notation.

Example, using Chafer as above:

Major Bible themes	Systematic theology
230	230
Cha	Cha
m	s

If you wish to note a new, revised, abridged or other change in the edition of a book, that change may be indicated below the author number as 2d ed., rev., abr., or you may use the new copyright date below the author number

An important exception to the rule to use the author's family name as the author number is in classifying biographies. Many small libraries use the designation B for biography, while others use the general number 920 or 92. It is essential that all biographies about one person are arranged together on the shelves. The books should be marked by the family name of the **person written about**, that is, the subject of the biography, not the author of the book, unless it is an autobiography. If you assign a Cutter number for biography, use the family name of the person written about and follow the Cutter number with the first letter of the author's family name in capitals, for you may have many biographies about a prominent person. When you do not use the Cutter number, use the first three letters of the family name of the person written about and on the line below, put the first letter of the author's family name in capitals.

Example: Biographies of Adoniram Judson

```
    920           920            Judson, Edward
    J92J    or    Jud              Life of Adoniram Judson.
                  J

    920           920            Wayland, Francis
    J92W    or    Jud              A memoir of the life and labor
                  W                of Adoniram Judson.
```

Works of criticism are another exception to the rule. You may want to keep critical works about an author or about a specific title with the works by the author. This may be done by using as the author number or Cutter number, the family name of the person discussed in the critical work. Use the capital letter Z as a symbol for a critical discussion of an author or work. After the Z, add the first letter of the author's family name. For a criticism of an individual work, the symbol Z and letter for the author's name may be added to the call number for the specific title.

Example: Critical works on John Bunyan

```
    823.42        823.42         Greaves, Richard L
    B94Zg   or    Bun              John Bunyan.
                  Zg

    823.42        823.42         Talon, Henri Antoine
    B94Zt   or    Bun              John Bunyan; the man and
                  Zt               his works.

    823.42        823.42         Kaufmann, U        Milo
    B94pZk  or    Bun              The pilgrim's progress and
                  pZk              tradition in Puritan meditation.
```

Current fiction is not classified in most small libraries, but the symbol "F" or "Fic" is used, placing the author number or Cutter number below the "F" or "Fic". Classic fiction, such as Dickens, Hawthorne or other well-known authors whose fiction is considered literature, is classified with the literature of the author's nationality.

When you make special decisions concerning classification, such as whether to use 920 or B for biography, write that decision in the margin of your classification book. This will not only help you to be consistent in your classification, but will be of assistance to another librarian who follows you as a cataloger. The classification book in which you have written the record of policy decisions become the guide book for classification for your library.

Final Steps in Classification

After you add the author number and work mark to the classification number, check the completed call number in the shelf list to be sure that another title on the subject does not have the same call number. If there is another book with the same number, make the necessary changes in the author number or Cutter number. If the Cutter number is the same although the names of the authors are different, extend the Cutter number.

Example: Books by Haines and Hainey

Haines	242				
	H153f		242		242
		or	Haines		Hainey
			f		d
Hainey	242				
	H1537d				

If you have a second title by an author beginning with the same letter of the alphabet, add an extra letter to the work mark. For example, if you have the book *Some important doctrines* by Chafer in 230   and you add
                                                                                        C433s
the title *Systematic theology* by Chafer, the call number would be 230
                                                                                                               C433sy

Check your work slip to be certain that the call number is correct. Make a temporary work slip giving the call number, author and title. Place this temporary work slip in the shelf list in order to prevent duplication of a call number while the cards are being prepared and filed. When the shelf-list card is filed, destroy the temporary slip.

Pencil the call number in the book on the back of the title page or on the page after the title page. Some libraries also write the call number and accession number in the top left corner of the back cover for use in circulation checking, to make certain the circulation cards belong to that particular book.

8. PREPARATION OF BOOKS AND CARDS

After a book is cataloged and classified, it must be prepared for the shelves and for circulation. The preparation includes typing the catalog cards, book pocket and card; adding ownership marks and circulation aids (book pocket and card, date due slip); covering the book jacket; lettering the spine of the book.

TYPING CARDS

If possible, use a typewriter with elite type. If you do not have a typewriter, use a pen with a fine point and permanent ink. Catalog cards, preferably medium weight, 3 × 5 inches (7.5 × 12.5 cm.), with a center hole at bottom of the card, may be purchased from a library supply house. Use a steel eraser or single edge razor blade with a bar top for correcting errors. You will also need pencil and ink erasers and a typing eraser.

Rules for Main Entry Cards

Make all of your cards as neat as possible. DO NOT strike over a letter, but erase errors. If there are too many errors, start a new card.

Indentations. In order to keep the cards uniform, set the margin two spaces from the left edge of the card and set the tabs as follows:
First indentation - 10 spaces from the left edge of the card;
Second indentation - 12 spaces from the left edge of the card;
Third indentation - 14 spaces from the left edge of the card.
If you write the cards by hand, lightly rule the cards for indentation, or you may purchase lined cards. For handwritten cards, use the left edge of the card as the margin.
First indentation - 13/16 of an inch (2cm.) from the left edge;
Second indentation - 15/16 of an inch (2.5cm.) from the left edge;
Third indentation - 1 1/16 inch (3cm.)from the left side.

Spacing. Start typing at the fourth space (line) (1.5cm.) from the top of the card.

1. BETWEEN THE LINES
    Typed lines follow one another consecutively except:
    a. Leave one line between collation and notes.
    b. Leave at least two lines between the end of the cataloging information and tracings. If there is not enough space for the tracings, turn the card over so that the bottom of the card is at the top. Type the tracings one below the other two spaces in from the margin. Start about half way down the card so that the tracings may be read easily when the card is in the catalog.

```
                                 ○



      1. Church history.
      2. Reformation.
      I. Title
      (Series)
```

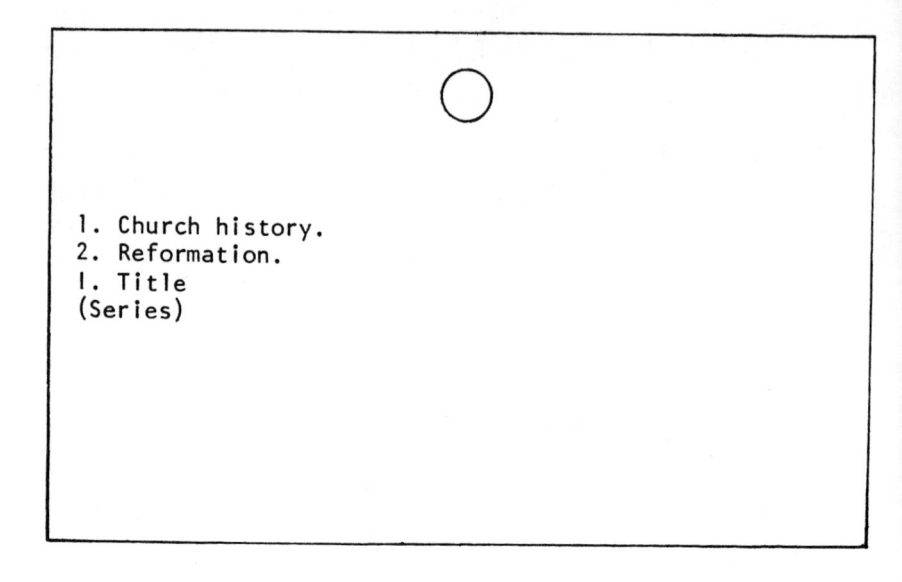

   2. BETWEEN ITEMS
      a. Leave one space after words, names, commas or semicolons.
      b. Leave two spaces after colons or periods.
      c. Leave two spaces between the different parts of the card, such as between title and imprint, or between paging and illustrations.
   3. INCOMPLETE INFORMATION
      a. Numbers - Leave one space for each digit of an incomplete number or date, as, 192 ; 19 .
      b. Name -   When information about a name is incomplete, leave eight spaces after the initial to allow for completion of the name when you find it, as Wilson, J   Edward Do not place a period after the initial.

Punctuation. Use punctuation marks as indicated below.
  1. PERIOD
     a. At the end of the title in the body of the card, as, Christian faith and modern theology. Ed. by Carl F.H. Henry.
     b. At the end of the edition statement; at end of imprint; at end of collation.
     c. Between subheadings of corporate author entry, as, France. Ministere des Affaires Etrangeres
     d. Do not use period:
        (1) After an author's name except when birth and death dates are included.
        (2) After a subject heading at the top of a subject card.
        (3) After a title followed by "by" when the author's name is repeated, as, The Christian church through the centuries, by James E. Jones and Jerome Eddy.
        (4) After parentheses, as, (Series)
        (5) After abbreviations of 1st, 2nd, 3rd, 4th, etc.

2. PERIOD AND DASH
   After a contents note, typed as period space hyphen space. For example, Contents. - The fall of Rome. - The rise of Greece.
3. COMMA
   a. Following the title before "by" and the author's name, when it is necessary to repeat the author's name as in joint authors.
   b. To separate the family name and the forename, as, Calvin, Jean.
   c. After the forename when a word is added, as, Henry, Carl, ed.
   d. Other cases following the usage of the language of your library.
4. SEMICOLON
   a. Subtitle, as, A new way of communication; Christian athletes today.
   b. Alternative title, as, Abraham; or, The obedience of faith.
   c. Several works in one volume where titles of all are on the title page.
   d. Between a series of numbers, as, 1915-1938; 1939-1942; 1943-1945.
5. PARENTHESES
   a. To enclose the series statement, as (Great events in church history)
   b. To enclose the word "Series" in the tracings, as, (Series)
6. HYPHEN AND/OR DASH
   a. Between dates use a single hyphen, as, 1872-1875; for inclusive paging, as p.97-103.
   b. In subject headings to indicate a subject subdivision use space hyphen space or double hyphen, as, MISSIONS - HISTORY or MISSIONS--HISTORY; or where a dash rather than a hyphen is part of the unit, as, War - who says so? or, War--who says so?
7. COLON
   To separate the page number of a bibliography from the word "Bibliography": as, Bibliography: p.126-134.
8. ELLIPSIS
   To show that you have omitted an unimportant part of a long title, as, Discourses on the Christian revelation . . . and astronomy.
   DO NOT USE DOUBLE PUNCTUATION, such as comma and dash, comma and parentheses, parentheses and period, period and comma, except after abbreviations.

Diacritical marks. Add by hand if your typewriter does not provide them. é, ç, ñ, ü

Capitalization. Follow the practice of the language of the work, except that a title is written like an ordinary statement. In English, capitalize only the first word and any proper nouns. Since in other languages, usage may vary, follow the usage of that language.

English: You are never alone
          The evolution of Christianity
          The last days of Jesus Christ
          A new look of September
German: Gemeinsame Leben
          Treue zur Welt
          Das Wesen der Kirche

Spanish: Elogio de la sombra
         Fervor de Buenos Aires
         Luna de enfrente y Cuaderno San Martin
         El otro, el mismo

The first word of all titles and all alternative titles preceded by "or" are capitalized, as, Apologetics; or, Christianity defensively stated.

Format of Card
1. CALL NUMBER
    Type at two spaces from the left edge of the card (margin), at the third line from the top so the author number is opposite the author's name. Type all sections of the call number, one below the other, as,
    >   973
    >   Aut
    >   v.1
2. AUTHOR
    a. PERSONAL NAME
       Type on the fourth line from the top of the card at the first indentation. Type the family name, comma, space, first name, space, middle name, comma, space, then the dates of birth and death, if used. Put a period after the dates, but do not put a period after the author's name if you do not use the dates.
          Garson, John Jerome, 1888-1967.
    b. CORPORATE NAME
       Type as written, on the fourth line at the first indentation. If the name is too long for the first line, continue on the line below, beginning at the third indentation.
          National Education Association. Committee on
             Government Relations.
3. BODY OF CARD
    a. TITLE
       Begin at the second indentation one line below the author's name and return to first indentation for all following lines. Type the title, including all information such as joint authors, editors, editions. If there is an alternate title, type the short title followed by a semicolon, the word "or", comma, and alternate title.
             The training of the twelve; or, Passages out of the Gospels,
          exhibiting the twelve disciples under discipline.
    b. IMPRINT
       The publishing information, which includes the place of publication, the publisher and date of publication or copyright date, begins two spaces after the title transcription, in the same paragraph. Small "c" precedes the copyright date, as c1974, with no period and no space before date.
    c. COLLATION
       The physical description of the book, which includes the number of pages or volumes and illustrative material, begins at the second indentation one line below the end of the title paragraph and returns to first indentation for other lines as needed. No space is left between number of pages and p., as, 372p., nor between number

of volumes and v., as, 2v. The word "illus." follows two spaces after the paging.
  d. SERIES
  It is not necessary to use a series note in a small library unless there is a special series which you want to emphasize. The series note follows the collation on the same line. It begins three spaces after collation and is enclosed in parentheses. Return to the first indentation if it extends to a second line. Do not use capital letters in the series note except for the first word of the series and proper names. If the series is numbered or if there is a date in the series, type the number or date as given.
     372p. illus. (The Tyndale classics
  series, no.7)

4. NOTES
  Notes are sometimes added to give additional information about the book or to list its contents. If used begin two lines below the collation at second indentation. List each note as a separate item. If you use a contents note, the items are followed by a period and dash.
     Contents. - v.1 From 1776 to 1860. - v.2 From 1861
  to 1914. - v.3 From 1915 to 1973.
  If the book has a good bibliography, you may include a note stating "Bibliography" or "Includes bibliographies" or you may include the paging, as,
     Bibliography: p.147-153.

5. TRACINGS
  Type tracings, which are indications for entries used on additional cards, only on the main entry and the shelf-list card. Leave at least two lines between the rest of the card and the tracings. They may be arranged in paragraph form, starting at the second indentation, or on the back of the card in a column, one below the other. Number each item in sequence, subject headings first, using arabic numerals, then added entries, using roman numerals. Series, the final tracing, is placed in parentheses: (Series)
         As a paragraph:
         1. Church history.   2. Missions - History.
         I. Jones, James Edwin, jt.auth.   II.Title. (Series)
         As a column:
         1. Church history
         2. Missions - History
         I. Jones, James Edwin, jt.auth.
         II. Title
         (Series)

6. CROSS REFERENCES
  Cross references, called "see" and "see also" references, are typed as follows:
     The term not used is typed on the third line from the top of the card at the second indentation. Two lines below at the third indentation, type the word "See" or "See also". Two lines below this at

the first indentation, type the term or name which is used. When several terms are referred to, type them alphabetically, one below the other. If subjects, the terms are all in capital letters.

Typing a Set of Cards

Some libraries type cards for added entries which are identical to the main entry card, but this involves so much typing and checking of each card that it is not recommended for small libraries. Instead of typing all cards in complete form, type only the main entry and shelf-list cards in full. For added entries, except title, type only the call number, author's name in full, short title, publisher and date. For the title card, type the call number, title at top of the card and author's name.

If you have access to a photocopying machine or a duplicating machine, photocopy the main entry card to make as many copies as needed for added entries. Type the added entry information on the cards.

MAIN ENTRY CARD

```
270
Jon      Jones, James Edgar
 c          The Christian church through the centuries,
         by James E. Jones and Jerome Eddy.  New York,
         Harper, c1974.
             763p.  (Great aspects of civilization, no.7)

         Bibliography:  p.751-759.

         1. Church history.  2. Europe - Civilization.
         I. Eddy, Jerome William, jt.auth.  II. Title.
         (Series)
```

SHELF-LIST CARD

```
270
Jon    Jones, James Edgar
 c         The Christian church through the centuries,
       by James E. Jones and Jerome Eddy.  New York,
       Harper, c1974.
           763p.  (Great aspects of civilization, no.7)

           Bibliography: p.751-759.

           1. Church history.  2. Europe - Civilization.
       I. Eddy, Jerome William, jt.auth.  II. Title.
       (Series)

7632  2.00  7-17-74         ◯
```

ADDED ENTRY - SUBJECT CARD

```
270         CHURCH HISTORY
Jon         Jones, James Edgar
 c              The Christian church through the centuries.
            Harper, c1974.
```

ADDED ENTRY - SUBJECT CARD

```
270         EUROPE - CIVILIZATION
Jon         Jones, James Edgar
 c              The Christian church through the centuries.
            Harper, c1974.
```

ADDED ENTRY - JOINT AUTHOR

```
270      Eddy, Jerome William, jt.auth.
Jon      Jones, James Edgar
c          The Christian church through the centuries.
         Harper, c1974.
```

ADDED ENTRY - TITLE CARD

```
270      The Christian church through the centuries
Jon      Jones, James Edgar
c
```

ADDED ENTRY - SERIES CARD

```
270      Great aspects of civilization, no.7
Jon      Jones, James Edgar
c          The Christian church through the centuries.
         Harper, c1974.
```

CROSS REFERENCE CARD

CIVILIZATION OF EUROPE

See

EUROPE - CIVILIZATION

PREPARING CIRCULATION CARDS

Book pockets and cards may be purchased from a library supply house. Some book pockets are available which have a date due slip on the pocket, with additional date due slips available to paste over the one on the pocket when it is filled.

Type the call number at the top left edge of the pocket. Type the author's name next to the call number, with the title below the author's name. Type the accession number at the top right edge of the pocket. If you purchase book cards, type the call number and accession number in the same position as on the book pocket. A line is marked for author and title on the purchased cards. If there is no author, the form of the main entry card is used on the pocket and book card. Stamp the book pocket with your library identification stamp.

```
270    Jones, James E.       7632
Jon    The Christian church
c      through the centuries
```

You can make a corner pocket by using heavy paper five inches (13 cm.) square. Fold the paper diagonally. Cut along the fold, making two pockets. You may cut off the corner, if desired.

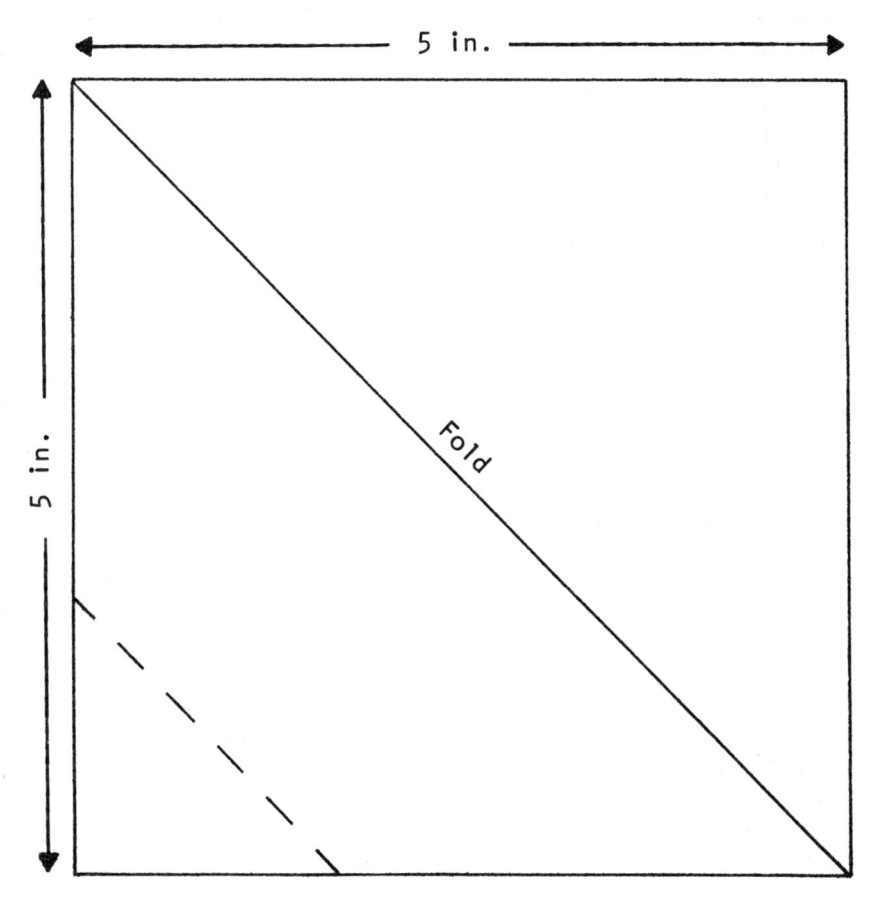

It is possible to cut envelopes in half and use the two halves for book pockets. Make sure they are securely pasted in the book.

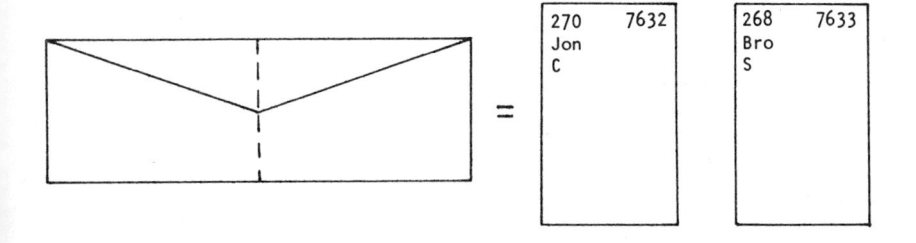

Book cards may be made by using 3 × 5 (7.5 × 12.5 cm.) cards. Leave one inch at the top for book information. Draw two lines across the card 5/16 inch (1 cm.) apart. Draw a line the length of the card from the first line to the bottom of the card, 5/8 inch (1.5 cm.) from the left edge of the card. Draw lines across the card approximately 5/16 inch (1 cm.) apart to the bottom of the card. Write "Due" in the small box on the first line. Write "Borrower" in the larger box.

270	Jones, James E.	7632
Jon	The Christian church	
c	through the centuries	

DUE	BORROWER

The book pocket and card should be typed at the time the catalog cards are typed. Place them in the book with the catalog cards for a final check of all typing or writing.

Date due slips may also be made if they are not purchased from a library supply house. Draw lines on a 3 × 5 inch (7.5 × 12.5 cm.) slip of paper as shown below:

DATE	DUE	

ADDING CIRCULATION AIDS

Add ownership marks if this was not done when the book was accessioned. Use a rubber stamp with the name and address of the library. Stamp the ownership mark on the book pocket (if not done previously) and on the bottom or top edges of the book pages while the book is held closed. It is not necessary to stamp any inside pages.

Paste the pocket into the book. Pockets may be purchased which are pregummed and need only to be moistened with water. If you do not have this type, paste around the four edges of the pocket and place the pocket on the page facing the back cover of the book. Place the pocket in the center between the two sides of the page, slightly lower than center when measured from the top of the page. Press firmly to insure its sticking and remove any excess paste with a soft cloth. The date due slip may be pasted over the lower part of the pocket. If you make your pocket, paste as above if made from an envelope, or if made from a diagonal piece of paper, paste to page facing inside back cover, toward left hand bottom corner. Paste date due slip on same page above pocket. Some libraries prefer to place the book pocket and date due slip in the front of the book on the page facing the front cover. Whichever you decide to do, always be consistent and place them in the same location in each book, unless there are important charts or maps on the chosen page. In that case, place them on the next blank page inside the cover.

Label the spine of the book with the call number. Put the call number the same distance from the bottom of all books in order that the books will look neat on the shelves and the number can be seen and located easily. Make a guide card with lines to show where the classification number and author letters should be located. Start the call number about 1½ inches (4 cm.) from the bottom of the spine. On a thin book, the lettering or label may be placed lengthwise of the book.

If you are able to obtain it, an electric stylus and transfer paper make a very satisfactory way to mark the spine. However, black india ink or white ink, depending on the color of the spine, may be used. Usually the sizing on the book cover must be removed before the transfer paper or ink will adhere. This may be done by painting over the areas with alcohol, ammonia, or book lacquer. After the lettering has been marked, cover it with a thin coat of book lacquer to preserve the lettering.

If the book has a paper jacket, a label should be affixed to the jacket. Type or write the label before pasting to the jacket. Some libraries prefer using a label for all books instead of lettering with a stylus or pen. Sometimes the labels do not adhere well, so additional paste may be needed. The label should then be covered with book lacquer.

Transparent jackets, made of acetate or mylar, placed over the paper book jackets, preserve the colorful and attractive paper jackets and protect the binding of the book, adding extra life to the circulation of the book. The jackets are available in various sizes. Some are available on rolls, with paper backing, and are adjustable to the size of the paper jacket. The jackets may be attached to the book with transparent tape or by gluing. If they are taped, they may be easily removed for display on bulletin boards. The tape may become dry, loosen, and must be replaced occasionally.

FINAL STEPS IN BOOK PREPARATION

1. Make final check of catalog cards, pocket, book card, lettering on spine, to be sure that all are correct and without error.
2. Remove catalog cards from the book and send the book to the shelves to be circulated or to the new book shelf for display.
3. Add to any statistics being kept.
4. Separate the catalog cards for filing:
   a. Shelf-list cards - to be filed in shelf-list file.
   b. Catalog cards - to be filed in card catalog.
      (1) Dictionary catalog - cards are arranged in one alphabet.
      (2) Divided catalog - author and title cards in one alphabet.
           - subject cards in another alphabet.
   c. Alphabetize the cards for filing.
5. Filing
   a. Cards are inserted in the catalog drawers where the filer thinks they should go, leaving them standing above the rod.
      (1) Shelf-list cards are filed by call number.
      (2) Catalog cards are filed following filing rules.
   b. Revise the filing. Check to be sure all cards are in the correct place and then drop the cards by removing the rod so they can fall down and join the others. If you do the first filing, leave if for a while and check it later to be sure you did not make a mistake. It is better if one person files the cards and another checks the filing.

9. FILING IN THE CARD CATALOG

THE CARD CATALOG

The card catalog is the most important reference tool in the library, for it is the index to the contents of the library. It is a file of cards which give information about each book in the library, including location. A library may start by using cardboard boxes for the card catalog, but since the catalog should be used by all patrons, a sturdy wood or metal case with standard size drawers to accommodate 3" x 5" (7.5 cm x 12.5 cm) cards should be purchased. The drawers should have a bottom center rod which will go through centered holes at the bottom of the cards. This rod is needed to prevent library patrons from removing or mixing up the cards or to prevent spilling if the drawer is dropped. The catalog should be placed where it will be most convenient for the use of your patrons.

In order for the cards to be used easily, the drawers or trays of the catalog should not become overcrowded. It is a good practice to fill the trays no more than two-thirds full so that there will be adequate space for the user to push the cards back and forth and examine them easily. It is desirable to place a blank card in the front and back of each tray to prevent the first and last cards from becoming soiled

The front of the trays should be labeled so the user can readily find the tray which holds the card for which he is looking. There should be a guide card (a card projecting above the catalog cards with words or letters to indicate the material directly behind it) placed between approximately every inch (2.54 cm) of tightly held catalog cards. Words on the guide cards should be short and simple. As much as possible, use half-cut guides, alternating right and left-hand ones.

There are two main types of card catalogs. In a *dictionary catalog,* all author, title, series and subject cards are filed together in alphabetical order. In a *divided catalog,* author, title and series cards are filed in alphabetical order in one catalog or section and subject cards are filed in alphabetical order in a separate catalog or section. Most small libraries use a dictionary catalog. If your library later decides to have a divided catalog, it should not be difficult to remove the subject cards and place them in a separate catalog.

In order for the card catalog to be effective, the cards must be arranged according to a definite plan, with the rules for filing carefully and consistently followed. The following rules apply to filing in the Roman alphabet. As your library becomes larger, you may find that you need more help with your filing. The following rules are based on *ALA rules for filing catalog cards* published by the American Library Association.
(See the bibliography, p. 127 for suggestions for complete books on filing.)

61

RULES FOR FILING CARDS

General Rules
1. **Alphabetize by entry word.** Alphabetize and file all catalog cards by the first word or name at the top of the card, that is, the "entry" word, whether it is an author, a title or a subject, excluding a beginning article (a, an, the) in all languages. This is a simplified arrangment which varies slightly from ALA filing rules.

    Love   (title)
    Barber, Lawrence Finley

    LOVE   (subject)
    DeBoer, Hans A

    Love   (title)
    Nestle, Bradley Michael

    Love, Albert Thatcher   (author)
    Love and marriage   (title)
    LOVE, CHARLES HASTINGS   (subject)
    Love, Frederick Robbins   (author)
    LOVE IN LITERATURE   (subject)
    Love in the New Testament   (title)
    The love of God   (title)
    LOVE POETRY   (subject)
    Love, sin and suffering   (title)
    LOVE (THEOLOGY)   (subject)
    Love without a limit   (title)

2. **Word by word.** Arrange word by word, beginning with the first word on the top line of the card. If there are two cards with the same first word, arrange by the second word. If the first and second words are the same, arrange by the third word, or as far as necessary to find a difference. Alphabetize letter by letter within the word.

    Foundations, a statement of Christian belief
    Foundations and frontiers of music education
    Foundations for teaching
    Foundations of Bible history
    Foundations of Christianity
    Foundations of the Christian faith
    Foundations of the English church
    Foundations of the faith

3. **Articles and prepositions.** Regard every word in the entry, including articles and prepositions, except for initial articles (a, an, the) in all languages. When an entry at the top of the card begins with an article, file by the word following.

Basic evangelism
A basic history of the United States
The basic ideas of Calvinism
Basic introduction to the New Testament

For a world like ours
For God was with them
For missionaries only
Forcey, Clark Johnson
Ford, Arthur
The forest people

In and around the book of Daniel
In Christ
In the arena
The incarnation

Miscellaneous theological works
A miscellany of American Christianity
Mischel, Walter
Les miserables
The Mishnah, oral teachings of Judaism

4. **Punctuation.** Ignore all punctuation, parentheses, accents and other diacritical marks. ç is filed as c; ü as u. File elisions, contractions and possessives as written. Do not supply missing letters, e.g., don't is filed as "dont", rather than as "do not"; it's is filed as "its", not as "it is".

Don Quixote
Donaldson, Frances
DONNE, JOHN
Don't look now
Don't sleep through the revolution
Dooley, Thomas Anthony
Doorways to devotion
Doran's minister's manual

Hawthorne, Nathaniel
He gave some prophets
Healing and Christianity
HEAVEN
Help! I'm a camp counselor
Henry, Carl Ferdinand
Here's how to win souls
He's coming again

It all depends
It can happen between Sundays
It took a miracle
Italian art

Italy, eternal land
It's a woman's privilege
It's dynamite
It's worth your life
Ivan Spencer

5. **Initials.** File a letter, single-letter word, or initial at the beginning of the letter before words beginning with that letter.

AAA
The ABC of Communism
ABC's of successful programs
A. J. Gordon
A. M. Mackay, pioneer missionary
AV instruction
Aaron, Daniel
Abandoned to Christ
ABELARD, PETER

ICR studies, No. 2
IGY: year of discovery
IQ and racial differences
I am a Christian
Ibsen, Henrik
I'd do it again
Ida S. Scudder of Vellore
Idea book for young people's leaders

6. **Acronyms.** File acronyms, such as Unesco, as words, unless written in capitals with periods or spaces between the letters.

Understanding ourselves and others
The undivided vision
The unequal yoke
UNESCO guide to science information
The unfolding message of the Bible
UNITED NATIONS

7. **Abbreviations.** File abbreviations (Dr., Mr., St., Gt. Brit.) as if spelled in full (Doctor, Mister, Saint or Street, Great Britain) in the language of the entry.

Doctor among Congo rebels
A doctor carries on
Dr. David Fielding's question box (Doctor)
Doctor Hudson's secret journal
Doctor in Bolivia
Dr. Livingstone, I presume?
The doctrine of the atonement
Doktor Taussig ist hier

The sabbath for man
Sacred books of the world
The saint and his Savior
St. Augustine of Hippo
St. Francis of Assisi
SAINT, NATHANIEL
St. Paul's epistles to the Corinthians
Salk, Lee
Salt of the earth

Exception: File Mrs. as written, but file Mr. as "Mister". The figure "&" (ampersand) is filed as "and" in the language of the entry.

Miss Terri
The mission and expansion of Christianity
MISSIONS
Mr. Audubon's Lucy   (Mister)
Mister Johnson
Mr. Jonathan Edwards
Mistress Masham's repose
Mitchell, Curtis
Monsieur et Madame Curie
M. & Mme. Pierot   (Monsieur et Madame)
Mrs. Howard Taylor
M'sieu Jean   (filed as spelled)
Mudge, Horace Granfell

Exception: In an author (main) entry, disregard prefix titles (Dr., Sir, Gen., Capt.) except to distinguish between persons. Example, Churchill, Winston, 1871-1947. Churchill, Sir Winston L 1874-1965.

8. **Hyphenated words.** File hyphenated words as separate words when the two parts are complete forms and each part can stand alone as a word. File hyphenated words as one word when it begins with a prefix such as anti-, bi-, co-, ex-, inter-, pan-, post-, etc. This applies whether the word is written with or without a hyphen.

Angel of the battlefield
Ann Judson
Answered or unanswered?
An anthology of verse
ANTI-CATHOLICISM
The antichrist
The antiquities of Jordan
ANTI-SEMITISM
The anxiety of influence

Post, Emily
Post-Christianity in Africa
Posthistoric man
The posthumous papers of the Pickwick Club
POST-MILLENNIALISM
POSTERS

　　　　Postgate, Raymond William
　　　　The postman of Patmos
　　　　Post-Reformation spirituality
　　　　The post-symbolist period

　　　　The sound and the fury
　　　　Sound currency
　　　　Sound-film reproduction
　　　　SOUND REPRODUCTION
　　　　Sound spending
　　　　SOUND-WAVES

9. **Compound words.** When compound words are written several ways, that is as two separate words, or hyphened, or as a single word, interfile all entries under the one-word form. Make a reference under the two-word form.

　　　　　　　　Every (as first word title)
　　　　In titles beginning "Every" the word "Every" is filed as a separate word whether it is printed separately or as a compound word.
　　　　　　　　Everybody can know
　　　　　　　　Every Christian's job
　　　　　　　　The everyday Bible
　　　　　　　　Every day life in Bible times
　　　　　　　　Everyman
　　　　　　　　Every man his way
　　　　　　　　Everyone in the Bible

　　　　　　　　HAND
　　　　　　　　Hand-book
　　　　For titles beginning "Hand book" or "Hand-book" see Handbook (filed as one word)
　　　　　　　　The hand of God in history
　　　　　　　　A hand with a mission
　　　　　　　　Hand-book almanac for Alaska
　　　　　　　　Handbook for Christian believers
　　　　　　　　A handbook of Christian social ethics
　　　　　　　　Hand book of French verbs
　　　　　　　　Hand-book of Italian literature
　　　　　　　　HANDEL, GEORG FRIEDRICH

10. **Variant spellings.** Words spelled two or more ways are interfiled in one place. Choose the spelling applicable to your area and make a reference card from the form not used.

　　　　Archeology see Archaeology
　　　　Catalogue see Catalog
　　　　Colour see Color
　　　　Labour see Labor
　　　　Savior see Saviour

11. **Numerals.** Numerals and dates in titles are filed as if spelled out in the language of entry. They are not filed numerically. Spell as if spoken. Use "and" before the last element in compound numbers.

    Effective prayer
    Egermeier, Elsie Emilie
    Eichrodt, Walther
    Eight French classic plays
    800,000,000: the real China   (Eight hundred million)
    1857 in India   (Eighteen fifty-seven)
    88 evangelistic sermons   (Eighty-eight)
    Einstein, Albert

    Nilsen, Maria
    Nine great preachers
    999 curiosities   (Nine hundred and ninety-nine)
    Nine lectures on preaching
    1944: year of invasion   (Nineteen forty-four)
    19 gifts of the spirit   (Nineteen)
    1939: how the war began   (Nineteen thirty-nine)
    The nineteenth century
    95 theses   (Ninety-five)
    NINEVEH

12. **Names.** Names are filed as written. ALA filing rules recommend that all names beginning with M' or Mc be filed as if spelled Mac, but this is not recommended for small libraries

    Dead men tell tales
    De Beer, Gavin Rylands
    Debrunner, Albert
    De Camp, Lyon Sprague
    The decision makers
    De Haan, Martin Ralph
    Derber, Milton
    De Remer, Bernard Robinson

    Mabry
    MacAdams
    MACHINERY-HISTORY
    Machines for today
    MacPherson
    Mc Alpin
    M'Gregor
    Minton

    VANADIUM
    Van Aken, Robert
    VAN BUREN, PAUL MATHEWS

Vandera, Alonso
Van der Aa, Pieter
Vanderbilt, Dorothy
Van der Veer, Judy
Van Derveer, Lettie C.

13. **Given names.** If a given name (forename or first name) is used by several people, file alphabetically if possible. If a descriptive phrase follows the given name, file alphabetically. For kings and popes, etc., the numeral is ignored unless all other designation is the same for two or more people, in which case arrange chronologically, earliest first.

    The Charles   (title)
    Charles, Abraham Scholl   (family name)
    Charles, Count of Burgundy   (given name)
    Charles Dickens   (title)
    Charles G. Finney   (title)
    Charles, Robert Henry   (family name)
    Charles I, emperor of Germany   (given name)
    Charles IV, emperor of Germany   (given name)
    Charles I, king of Great Britain   (given name)
    Charles II, king of Great Britain   (given name)
    Charles V and the people   (Charles the fifth -title)

    John Adams and the American Revolution
    JOHN, APOSTLE
    JOHN BIRCH SOCIETY
    John Bunyan in relation to his times
    John: life eternal
    John looks at the cross
    John of Salisbury
    John XXIII, Pope
    JOHN THE BAPTIST

14. **Author entries**

    A. File author cards by the family name and then by the given name. If you know only the initials of given names for some authors, place the cards for these before other given names beginning with the same letter.

        Brown, A   I
        Brown, Arlo

    Brown, Arthur Edward
    Brown, H   C
    Brown, Harold Ogden
    Brown, L   M
    Brown, Leslie
    Brown, W   Norman
    Brown, William

B. Interfile alphabetically by title all works by an author, whether main or added entries. For added entries, disregard the author main entry and file by title of main entry.

    Shakespeare, William
    Thayer, William Roscoe
      The best Shakespearean plays

    Shakespeare, William
      Four great comedies

    Shakespeare, William
      King Lear

    Shakespeare, William
      Macbeth

    Shakespeare, William
      Plays and sonnets

      Shakespeare, William, jt. author
    Fletcher, John
      The two noble kinsmen

C. If you have the same work as title of a book and as title of an analytic (See chapter 6, p.31), file title of the book first.

    Shakespeare, William   (author and title)
      As you like it

    Shakespeare, William   (author and title analytic)
      As you like it
    Thayer, William Roscoe
      The best Shakespearean plays

D. File an author and title analytic first by author, then by title, then by main entry.
    Shakespeare, William
      Midsummer night's dream
    Bettencourt, Albert Saxon
      Comedies of note

69

Shakespeare, William
Midsummer night's dream
Harper, David George
Four pleasant plays

E. File a criticism of a work after the entry for the work.

Shakespeare, William   (author and title)
King Lear

SHAKESPEARE, WILLIAM. KING LEAR   (subject criticism)
Smith, Gordon Ross
Essays on Shakespeare

F. File subject cards for a book **about** an author after all of the works **by** him. File second by the author of the book, then by title.
G. File editions of the same work chronologically by date or number, with earliest edition first. File the ones with no number or date before the numbered or dated editions

15. **Title entries**
    A. If you have more than one work with the same title, arrange by author.
    B. If you have more than one edition of the same work, arrange by publication date, the earliest date first. Some libraries, however, use only the title card for the latest edition or best edition. This card may be marked "Other editions under author", for you will have an author card for each edition. The single title card takes care of all editions, even though editors, translators, and publishers of the various editions may differ. The same rule holds for other added entries, e.g., cards for compilers, editors, translators, as well as for subject cards.
    C. If you have the same work as title of a book and as title of an analytic, file title of the book first.

16. **Subject entries**
    A. File a subject without subdivision, arranged alphabetically by main entry.
    B. File subjects with date and period subdivision chronologically, the earliest first and the most inclusive period before shorter periods within the inclusive period. Periods denoted by words (-REVOLUTION) or by words and dates (-RESTORATION, 1814-1830) are arranged chronologically, not alphabetically.
       FRANCE-HISTORY
       FRANCE-HIST.-MEDIEVAL PERIOD, 987-1515
       FRANCE-HIST.-HOUSE OF VALOIS, 1328-1589

FRANCE-HIST.-BOURBONS, 1589-1789
FRANCE-HIST.-18th CENTURY
FRANCE-HIST.-REGENCY, 1715-1723
FRANCE-HIST.-REVOLUTION, 1789-1799
FRANCE-HIST.-CONSULATE AND EMPIRE, 1799-1815
FRANCE-HIST.-RESTORATON, 1814-1830
FRANCE-HIST.-20th CENTURY

17. **Reference Cards**
    A. File "see" references in their place alphabetically. Disregard the words "see" and "see also" and the words following them when filing.

    Tuttle, William M
    Twaddell, William Freeman
    Twain, Mark   See   Clemens, Samuel Langhorne
    Tweedie, Donald Francis

    B. File a "see also" reference or an history card (explaining change of name of a country, organization, periodical, etc.) before the first entry under the same word or words, whether the entry is a subject or a title.

    DEAD SEA SCROLLS   See also QUMRAN COMMUNITY
    DEAD SEA SCROLLS
    DEAD SEA SCROLLS-RELATION TO THE N.T.

Bible Entries
There are two different methods of filing Bible entries which are recommended in this manual. Many small libraries prefer to arrange Bible entries in straight alphabetical order word by word, disregarding the kind of entry, form of heading and punctuation. It may be advisable to follow this method if your patrons are not well acquainted with the order of the books of the Bible as given in the Authorized (King James) Version. Many Bible schools, Bible colleges and seminaries, however, prefer to arrange Bible entries in the order of the books of the Bible. Rules for both methods are given in detail in this manual. Choose whichever method you think best for your library and be consistent in using it.

Alphabetic arrangement. File Bible entries alphabetically as follows:
1. Entries for Bible, the sacred book, follow entries for the family name Bible.
2. Arrange Bible entries in straight alphabetical order word by word, disregarding kind of entry, form of heading and punctuation.
3. File headings which include a date alphabetically up to the date, then arrange the same headings with different dates
   chronologically by date, earliest first.

71

4. File different kinds of entries which have the same headings in groups in the following order.
   A. Main or added entries subarranged alphabetically by title.
   B. Subject subarranged alphabetically by main entry.
5. File entries for chapters and verses in numerical order after all entries for the whole book. A larger part beginning with the same chapter precedes a smaller part. Verses under the same chapter are arranged numerically by the first number.
6. Numbered books of the Bible follow in numerical order the same name used collectively without number. File as follows:
   A. Headings for the whole, with all its main entry and subject subdivisions alphabetically
   B. Headings for numbered books, in numerical order, each arranged in two groups as follows:
      (1) Alphabetical - for author and subject subdivisions
      (2) Numerical - for chapters and verses

   BIBLE. N.T. CORINTHIANS -COMMENTARIES
   Bible. N.T. Corinthians. English. 1961
   BIBLE. N.T. I CORINTHIANS -COMMENTARIES
   Bible. N.T. I Corinthians. English. 1958
   BIBLE. N.T. 1 CORINTHIANS 10-11 -COMMENTARIES
   BIBLE. N.T. 2 CORINTHIANS - COMMENTARIES

7. File the abbreviations "N.T." and "O.T." when followed by a subheading, as "New Testament" and "Old Testament".

   The following examples cover the rules given above:

   Bible, John Harvey
   Bible, Mary Ernestine
   BIBLE
   Bible, Acts, **see** Bible. N.T. Acts
   BIBLE AND SCIENCE
   BIBLE-ANTIQUITIES
   Bible. Apocrypha, **see** Bible. O.T. Apocrypha
   Bible biographies
   BIBLE-BIOGRAPHY
   Bible. English. 1912
   Bible. English. American Revised. 1966
   Bible. English. Authorized. 1938
     The Holy Bible containing the Old and New Testaments
   Bible. English. Authorized. 1938
     The Oxford self-pronouncing Bible
   Bible. English. Authorized. 1949
   Bible. English. Authorized. Selections. 1941
   Bible. English. Authorized. Selections. 1958
   BIBLE. ENGLISH -BIBLIOGRAPHY
   BIBLE. ENGLISH -HISTORY
   Bible. English. Revised standard. 1956

BIBLE - ENGLISH - VERSIONS
Bible. Greek. Codex Sinaiticus
The Bible in art
BIBLE IN LITERATURE
BIBLE- MANUSCRIPTS
BIBLE. N.T. ACTS -BIOGRAPHY
Bible. N.T. Acts. English. Authorized. 1959
Bible. N.T. Acts. English. Barclay. 1957
BIBLE. N.T. -COMMENTARIES
Bible. N.T. English. American revised. 1959
Bible. N.T. Epistles. English. Phillips. 1957
Bible. N.T. Epistles of John. English. Barclay. 1960
Bible. N.T. Philippians
Bible. O.T. Hebrew. 1960
Bible. O.T. Psalms. English. 1943
BIBLE. O.T. RUTH - COMMENTARIES
BIBLE - PARAPHRASES
Bible. Philippians, **see** Bible. N.T. Philippians
BIBLE STORIES
Bible. Zechariah, **see** Bible. O.T. Zechariah

Canonical arrangement. File Bible entries in Bible (King James Version) order as follows:

1. Bible manuscripts, both language and subject
2. Complete Bible, by language
3. Complete Bible, by subject
4. Parts of the Bible in canonical order:
   A. Complete Old Testament
      (1) By language
      (2) By subject
   B. Individual books of the Old Testament
      (1) By language
      (2) By subject
   C. Complete New Testament
      (1) By language
      (2) By subject
   D. Individual New Testament books
      (1) By language
      (2) By subject

Explanation of this arrangement.
1. You probably will not have any actual manuscripts, but if you do, file the cards first alphabetically by the language of the manuscript. Under each language, file the complete Bible, then the part of the Bible (KJV order). Under each part, arrange alphabetically by name of the manuscript.
2. Complete Bible. Printed polyglot (multiple language) editions of the Bible precede all other language editions. Other texts of the complete Bible

are arranged alphabetically by language. Entries for dialects of the Bible are made by adding the name of the dialect in parentheses after the name of the language.

>Bible. French (Old French)
>Bible. French (Vaudois)

Under each language, if you have several editions, file first the straight text, then by the name of the version, then chronologically by the date. If the text is a paraphrase or selections, the proper subheading "Selections" or "Paraphrase" follows the language and version in the heading, followed by the date.

Small libraries may choose to omit version or translator, but if you think your patrons would be interested in the designation of different versions, use the name of the version in the main entry.

3. Bible as subject. Subject entries for the complete Bible are filed after the entries for texts of the complete Bible and before entries for parts of the Bible. Subject entries for parts of the Bible are filed after texts for the corresponding parts.

>Bible. English. Authorized. 1942
>Bible. Spanish. Authorized. 1958
>BIBLE - ANTIQUITIES
>BIBLE - BIBLIOGRAPHY
>BIBLE - HISTORY
>Bible. O.T. Hebrew. 1943
>BIBLE. O.T. - COMMENTARIES
>BIBLE. O.T. - INTRODUCTIONS
>Bible. O.T. Genesis, French. 1964
>BIBLE. O.T. GENESIS - COMMENTARIES
>Bible. O.T. Psalms. Spanish. 1961
>BIBLE. O.T. PSALMS - COMMENTARIES
>Bible. N.T. Spanish. 1968
>BIBLE. N.T. - VERSIONS

4. Parts of the Bible. The arrangement for parts of the Bible is by the order of the books in the King James Version. A collective heading precedes the individual books which the heading encompasses. Collective headings are the names of groups of books, such as Pentateuch, O.T. Prophets, N.T. Gospels, Epistles of Paul, Catholic or General Epistles (James, 1 & 2 Peter, 1,2,3 John and Jude), Pastoral Epistles (1 & 2 Timothy, Titus).

>Bible. English. Authorized. 1942
>Bible. O.T. Hebrew. 1943
>BIBLE. O.T. PENTATEUCH -COMMENTARIES
>Bible. O.T. Genesis. French. 1964
>BIBLE. O.T. EXODUS - COMMENTARIES

Numbered books of the Bible follow numerically the same name used collectively without number.

    Bible. O.T. Kings
    Bible. O.T. 1 Kings
    Bible. O.T. 2 Kings

Entries for single chapters or several chapters follow entries for the whole book. The larger part beginning with the same chapter always precedes the smaller part.

    Bible. O.T. Psalms 1-51
    Bible. O.T. Psalms 1-40
    Bible. O.T. Psalms 1-20
    Bible. O.T. Psalms 1-10
    Bible. O.T. Psalm 1
    Bible. O.T. Psalm 2
    Bible. O.T. Psalm 23
    Bible. O.T. Psalm 119

The information in this chapter was adapted by permission of the American Library Association from *ALA Rules for Filing Catalog Cards,* copyright © 1968 by the American Library Association.

10. NONBOOK MATERIALS

Although books comprise the principal collection of your library, much valuable information is found in other print and nonprint formats. Today's library is not a book warehouse, but a media center for the housing and distribution of information in various forms. As such, it can be the stimulus for a variety of learning experiences by making available and encouraging the use of graphic and photographic materials, sound reproductions and three-dimensional objects, as well as the printed page.

Since all of these materials must be organized for use, detailed instructions are given for handling the various types of nonbook materials. In most cases, more than one method is given so that you may choose the one suitable to your library.

TEXTUAL MATERIALS

Pamphlets

Although pamphlets are described in library literature as booklets of fifty pages or less, much useful up-to-date material published in the form of brochures, single sheets or cards is also treated as pamphlets, organized by subject and filed in a cabinet called "Pamphlet File", "Information File" or "Vertical File". Pamphlets frequently are more popular with library users than books because they are brief and are often more up-to-date.

The procedures necessary in maintaining a pamphlet file are (1) a regular program for selection; (2) a simple, efficient order routine; (3) a basic, flexible subject heading system (classification); (4) a simple storage and circulation procedure; and (5) a frequent review of the files for discarding outdated and unused materials and for noting needs.

CRITERIA FOR SELECTION OF NONBOOK MATERIALS

POINTS OF QUALITY	POINTS OF INFERIORITY
(Accept)	(Reject)

LOOK FOR
AUTHENTICITY

Accurate facts	Inaccurate facts
Facts impartially presented	Facts distorted by bias
Up-to-date information	Fake revised version: date only changed, no up-dating of contents
Other acceptable works of producer	Consistent rejection of other works of producer

POINTS OF QUALITY	POINTS OF INFERIORITY
(Accept)	(Reject)

APPROPRIATENESS

Vocabulary at user's level	Vocabulary too easy or difficult
Concepts at user's level	Concepts too easy or difficult
Useful data	Extraneous data
Media-subject correlation (e.g., art prints to art, specimens to science)	Media does not add to subject communication
Titles, captions, etc. related to subject	Titles, captions, etc., confuse subject concepts
Narration, dialogue, sound effects related to subject	Narration, dialogue, sound effects unrelated to subject
Individual and/or group use suitability	Limited individual and/or group use suitability

SCOPE

Full coverage as indicated	Gaps in coverage
Superior concept development by this means	Better concept development by other means
Content to satisfy demands for current subjects	Irrelevance to current topics

INTEREST

Relationship to user's experience	No relationship to user's cultural environment
Intellectual challenge	No intellectual challenge
Curiosity satisfaction	No satisfactory answers
Credibility	Implausibility
Imagination appeal	Prosaic presentation
Human appeal	Negative human values
Sensory appeal	No stimulation

ORGANIZATION

Logical development	Confused development; excessive repetition
Pertinence of all sequences	Unrelated sequences
Balance in use of narration and dialogue; music and sound effects; background elements	Ineffective or overpowering use of the same elements

POINTS OF QUALITY	POINTS OF INFERIORITY
(Accept)	(Reject)

TECHNICAL ASPECTS

Tone fidelity	Tone distortion
Clarity	Extraneous sounds, visuals too detailed
Intelligibility	Difficulty in following image and/or sound
In-focus pictures	Fuzzy out-of-focus pictures
True size relationships	Unreal size relationships
Unified composition	Confused composition
Effective color use	Color is less effective than black and white
Complete synchronization of sound and image	Uneven synchronization of sound and image

SPECIAL FEATURES

Descriptive notes, teachers and/or users guide	Absence of useful notes, guides
Pertinent accompanying material	Unrelated materials packaged together

PHYSICAL CHARACTERISTICS

Ease in handling, for user, for storage	Difficulty in handling
Minimum instruction for individual use	Special training requirements for use
Attractive packaging	Unattractive packaging
Durability	Flimsy construction
Ease of repair	Difficulty in repairing damage

LIBRARY POTENTIAL

Relevancy that promotes communication	No furthering of communication
Flexibility for many effective uses	Features which limit use

SELECTION AIDS

Recommendation in evaluation sources	Rejection in evaluation sources

POINTS OF QUALITY	POINTS OF INFERIORITY
(Accept)	(Reject)

COST

Conformity to budget	Too costly for budget
No less expense for satisfactory substitutes	Satisfactory substitutes cheaper
Inexpensive or already purchased equipment	Expensive equipment needed
Economy if purchased	Greater expense to rent
Average supplemental costs for replacement, repair, physical processing, storage	Too expensive to replace, repair, process for use

Reprinted from *Developing Multi-Media Libraries* **by Warren B. Hicks and Alma M. Tillin by Permission of R. R. Bowker Company (A Xerox Education Company). Copyright© 1970 by Xerox Corporation.**

Selection. Follow the guidelines for book selection discussed in chapter four of this manual. See also "Criteria for Selection of Nonbook Materials" above.

Order routine. It is possible to obtain free material by visiting or writing to local health departments, physicians' offices, garden stores, police and fire departments, paint stores, etc., and asking for free booklets and brochures. Various offices, branches, or departments of local or national governments often have much material. By writing to them and asking that they send lists of available publications, you may obtain many valuable publications which are free or inexpensive.

Some libraries use the services of a purchasing agency to handle orders for pamphlets so that several may be ordered at one time and there will be one billing. Several agencies are listed in the bibliography of this manual. Frequently, purchasing agencies may give a small discount, but often the use of such an agency is more for convenience in mailing and billing than for per item cost savings.

In addition to material which is ordered, and free material which is requested, one can frequently use free material which is donated to the library or sent unsolicited. Some caution should be practiced, however, so that purely propagandistic literature is avoided.

Another source of material is magazines and newspapers which are donated to the library or which the library plans to discard. A careful scanning of such material will often reveal articles that can be clipped. These articles can then be assigned a subject heading and filed. The source and page number should be carefully written in the bottom margin or at the top of the article along with the date of the source. Use as complete bibliographical information as possible. Continued articles should be carefully collected and stapled together.

Some libraries mount the article on paper, but this is a time-consuming process which should be done only for articles which have historical value. If mounting is done, use a good grade of paper. Longer articles can be used just as they are. Small clippings are more easily filed if they are placed in envelopes. Several clippings on the same subject can be placed in one envelope with the subject heading written on the envelope, followed by the number of clippings.

The person in charge of the library can determine what needs to be clipped and indicate this on the front cover of the magazine or on an attached slip. A student assistant can do the actual clipping. If the librarian has no help, it probably is not advisable to spend much time clipping.

Classification and processing. An alphabetical file of subject headings is the most efficient method of arranging pamphlets, for it is direct and simple. Patrons can easily find material if you use subject headings which are clear and precise. Avoid the use of subdivisions and inverted headings as much as possible. You may prefer to start your pamphlet file by using broad headings, but your patrons will find specific headings more useful. If you have *Sears List of Subject Headings* or *Readers' Guide to Periodical Literature,* use one of them for pamphlet subject headings. Write in alphabetical sequence in the list any additional headings which you use.

In order to determine the subject of the pamphlet, it may be necessary to scan or read it, for titles are often misleading. If you have a pamphlet which covers one or more subjects, a broad subject heading may be used. If possible, try to obtain extra copies of the pamphlet or make a photocopy and file under more than one subject. If you do this, note on each pamphlet where you have filed other copies so that later you will be reminded that you have assigned another subject heading to it when you find the additional copy in your files.

When the subject is decided upon, write the subject in ink in the right or left corner of the pamphlet or across the top in the center. Always use the same position on all pamphlets. If the subject has not been used before, check (✓) it in the subject heading list.

The name of the library and the date of processing should be stamped or written in ink on each piece. In order not to clutter the top of the material, stamp the date on the bottom of the material, or on the right or left margin.

A card index to subject headings should be maintained. A single file drawer, placed on top of the pamphlet file, may contain cards showing all the headings used in the pamphlet file, as well as "See" and "See also" references.

"See" references are used to show that there is nothing under the subject, but the user should see another subject:

>PLAYS
>See
>DRAMAS

"See also" references are used to indicate that there are other similar or more specific subjects:

>ADOLESCENCE
>See also
>CHILD STUDY
>YOUTH

Keep your card index consistent by following the procedure for spacing and capitalization recommended in chapter eight.

Some libraries insert cards in the card catalog referring the user from the subject headings to the pamphlet file.
Example:

>CHILD STUDY
>See also
>Information File for additional material

Storage. A metal or wooden file cabinet, preferably legal size, is ideal for a pamphlet file, but if you do not have funds to buy filing cabinets, wooden or strong cardboard boxes may be used.

All materials under a subject should be placed in a manila folder. Small pamphlets may be placed upright in the folders and large ones horizontal. Use good quality folders, for cheap ones will deteriorate quickly. Subject headings may by written or typed on the filing tabs of the folders and then arranged alphabetically in the file. Metal tab guides for each letter of the alphabet are recommended, but not necessary.

Circulation. Few libraries use pockets and cards for vertical file material. A simple card may be made following a form similar to the following:

	PAMPHLETS		
Date Due	Borrower's Name	Subject	Amount
Jan. 4, 1978	Jean Patois	Baptism	2

Save the used envelopes in which you receive magazines and other materials and use them to hold pamphlets borrowed from the library. The envelope can then be stamped with the date due; the subject and the number of pamphlets can be written on it. If this system is used, patrons should be advised that they must return the pamphlets in the same envelope so that the date due will be available to the person working at the circulation desk.

Some libraries stamp the date due on the back of the pamphlet. When material is returned, the pamphlet card is taken from the circulation file and placed in a box or tray for reuse. Some libraries check off or rule through the previous circulation transaction.

A limit on the number of pamphlets allowed for one person to check out and the time period for circulation is a local matter. Most libraries have shorter loan periods for pamphlets since they are brief and can be used in less time than a book. Time should be determined by the use and the number of pamphlets available.

Maintenance and weeding. Frequent reviewing of the vertical files to determine need of more or new materials and to weed out old and worn material is necessary. Pamphlets that are worn and torn should be discarded. These can frequently be spotted when material is returned to the library and placed immediately in a box or shelf for reviewing rather than refiled.

Since one of the advantages of a pamphlet file is its being up-to-date, avoid leaving outdated material in the file. To file newer editions of works in a file with older editions is seldom a good practice. Some material does not go out of date, so you cannot arrive at an automatic weeding date, but you may decide to review material and consider discarding it if it is older than five to ten years. Larger files are weeded more rigorously than smaller ones. If the circulation practice of stamping date due on the material is used, one can check the use of the material as a consideration in weeding.

Serials

Serials are publications issued in consecutive parts at regular or irregular intervals and intended to continue indefinitely. A periodical is a serial with a distinctive title usually issued twice a year or more, with each issue containing articles by several people. "Journal" and "magazine" are words used for periodicals. A journal is considered more scholarly than a magazine. Newspapers are serials whose chief purpose is to publish news. Other forms of serials are yearbooks, annuals, transactions and proceedings of societies, and any series cataloged together instead of separately.

Periodicals

Selection and ordering. In selecting periodicals for your library, you should follow the guidelines described in chapter four on book selection. The religious periodicals indexed in *Christian Periodical Index* published by the Christian Librarians' Fellowship or in *Index to Religious Periodical Literature* published by the American Theological Library Association may be considered for purchase by your library. Your teachers and your library committee members may recommend periodicals. Carefully consider periodicals which are published locally or nationally, for they may interest your students more than those produced in another country.

Although it is possible to order periodicals directly from the publisher, this causes you to write many letters and to pay many bills. Many librarians place their orders for periodicals with a subscription agent who renews subscriptions each year. See the appendix for a list of agents.

To order periodicals from an agent, make an alphabetical list (in duplicate) of the periodicals you want to order through him. Ask him to order the periodicals you want to order through him. Ask him to order the periodicals to continue until further notice. You may cancel subscriptions at the end of any subscription period. The agent will send an itemized bill for all subscriptions. The agent will tell you whether you should write him or the publisher for missing issues. Keep a correspondence file on periodicals for reference in case you have a problem.

Recording procedure. For periodicals and newspapers, a checking card similar to those illustrated may be used to record each issue as received. Keep these cards in a periodical record file. These cards may be purchased from a library supply house for different publication frequencies (such as daily, weekly, monthly, quarterly) or you may make your checking cards by ruling lines on a plain card, preferably 4"x6", or have a local print shop print them for you. To record receipt, check (✓) under the appropriate date or write under the proper month the number of the issue. Information which should be typed or written on the checking card includes title, publisher, agent (if different from publisher), number of volumes per year, when the volume year begins, whether you will have the periodical bound and the promptness of receipt. It may be useful also to record whether an index is received, when it is received or where it is located if it is bound into the periodical. Some of this information may be placed on the back of the card.

At regular intervals, perhaps once a month, examine the checking cards to see if any issue is missing or is long overdue. Check your periodical shelves to see if the issue is there and was overlooked for checking when it was received. If issues are missing, write to the publisher or your periodicals agent. On the checking card, make a pencil notation of the date that a replacement request has been sent. When the issue is received, erase the penciled date and record the checking information.

Quarterlies frequently use a seasonal name instead of a month for the issues, e.g. Spring, Summer, Fall, Winter. Enter under the month applicable to that season.

Many publishers begin a volume in the middle of a year and carry the issues over into the next year. Indicate both volume numbers in the "Volume" column. The new volume number may also be placed over the entry for issue 1 of that volume.

Since most small libraries keep newspapers only 2 or 3 months, it is not necessary to keep a record of receipt. If you do keep a record, mark a card or notebook paper with the months of the year written in a column on the left with 31 spaces across the top for the days of the month. Check (✓) the proper space as each issue is received.

Handling and storage. Periodicals should be stamped with your ownership stamp. Select a location on the cover and be consistent in stamping all periodicals in the same place. Write the volume and issue number in the upper left corner in order to help in keeping the volumes in order when they are stored. Current issues of periodicals should be displayed, arranged alphabetically by title, in a special section of shelving or on a reading table. Store older issues alphabetically by title in a special storage section or room. Periodicals most valuable for reference may be kept for a definite number of years or permanently.

TITLE	TIME					FREQUENCY	Wkly	DAY DUE	Friday		TITLE PAGE
PUBLISHER OR AGENT	Time, Inc.						SUBSCRIP. DATE	9/4/70			
ADDRESS	Rockefeller Center, NY 10020						NOS. PER VOL.	26-27			INDEX
BOUND	No						VOLS. PER YEAR	2			

PREPARED							IN BINDERY							
YEAR	SER.	VOL.	JAN.	FEB.	MAR.	APR.	MAY	JUNE	JULY	AUG.	SEPT.	OCT.	NOV.	DEC.	T.P.	I.
1976	107	1	5	9	14	19	24	108:1	6	10	14	18	23		
	108	2	6	10	15	20	25	2	7	11	15	19	24		
		3	7	11	16	21	26	3	8	12	16	20	25		
		4	8	12	17	22	27	4	9	13	17	21	26		
		5		13	18	23		5				22			
1977	109	1	6	10	14	18	23	110:1	6	10	14	18	23		

TITLE	MOODY MONTHLY					FREQUENCY	Monthly	DAY DUE	25th		TITLE PAGE
PUBLISHER OR AGENT	Moody Press						SUBSCRIP. DATE	9/1/65			
ADDRESS	820 N. LaSalle St., Chicago, IL 60610						NOS. PER VOL.	11			INDEX
BOUND	Yes						VOLS. PER YEAR	1 - Sept.			

PREPARED							IN BINDERY							
YEAR	SER.	VOL.	JAN.	FEB.	MAR.	APR.	MAY	JUNE	JULY	AUG.	SEPT.	OCT.	NOV.	DEC.	T.P.	I.
1974	74/75	1	5	6	7	8	9	10	11	—	75:1	2	3	4	
1975	75/76	2	5	6	7	8	9	10	11	—	76:1	2	3	4	
1976	76/77	3	5	6	7	8	9	10	11	—	77:1	2	3	4	
1977	77/78	4	5	6	7	8	9	10	11	—	78:1	2	3	4	

TITLE	MISSIOLOGY					FREQUENCY	Qrtly	DAY DUE	Jan,Apr,Jly,Oct	TITLE PAGE
PUBLISHER OR AGENT	American Society of Missiology						SUBSCRIP. DATE	12/1/72		
ADDRESS	P.O. Box 1041, New Canaan, CT 06840						NOS. PER VOL.	4		INDEX
BOUND	Yes						VOLS. PER YEAR	1		
PREPARED	Supersedes PRACTICAL ANTHROPOLOGY									

YEAR	SER.	VOL.	JAN.	FEB.	MAR.	APR.	MAY	JUNE	JULY	AUG.	SEPT.	OCT.	NOV.	DEC.	T.P.	I.
1973	1	1	1			2			3			4				
1974	2	2	1			2			3			4				
1975	3	3	1			2			3			4				
1976	4	4	1			2			3			4				
1977	5	5	1			2			3			4				
1978	6	1	1			2										

MISSIOLOGY

Cards for recording receipt of periodicals

There are several methods for storing periodicals which you do not wish to bind. A volume may be wrapped in paper and tied with cord. Write the title, volume number and date on the back of the package. Another method is to label a piece of heavy paper with title, volume and date. Punch two holes so that the cord for tying the volume together will thread through the holes and hold the label in place. Keener Rubber Co. of Alliance, Ohio manufactures "H" bands of rubber in various sizes which are excellent for holding together a volume of periodicals. The "H" bands slip off and on easily when a periodical must be removed for reference. Several library supply houses sell special cardboard boxes in appropriate sizes to hold a volume of periodicals.

Binding. Periodicals which you wish to keep for reference should be bound or tied together. Scholarly periodicals should be bound if your budget permits. Use a reliable commercial binder if one is available. If not, someone on your staff could be taught to bind periodicals. To prepare periodicals for binding:

1. Assemble all of the issues of a volume. Be sure the volume number is the same for all issues and that no issues are missing. Do not bind if issues are missing. It is important to be careful about volume and issue number, for the volume may begin the middle of one year and end the following year.
2. Arrange in proper order with the first issue on top and the final issue on the bottom. As an additional check, look at the paging. Some periodicals are paged consecutively by numbering from page one of the first issue to final page of the last issue. It is advisable to leaf through each issue and tear out any loose coupons or advertising material. Be sure that you do not discard any page of text with the advertising.
3. Place the title page and table of contents on the top of the first issue. You may find the title page, table of contents and index at the end of the last issue of the volume. If the index is bound in the last issue, leave it there. If it is loose, place it on the bottom of the volume pile after the last issue.
4. In each volume, place a slip of paper giving instructions for lettering on the cover and color of binding. Give the title, date, the year only unless there is more than one volume in a year, volume number and part, if the volume is too large to bind as one volume and must be divided.

1972	1972	1972	1972	1972
v. 16	JAN-JUNE	JULY-DEC	JAN-JUNE	JULY-DEC
	v. 72	v. 73	v. 66	v. 66
		v. 73	pt. 1	pt. 2

5. After you have carefully checked to be sure that everything is correct, tie each volume with its instruction sheet into a bundle so that it will remain complete and in order until bound.

Cataloging. Most small libraries do not catalog periodicals. Some libraries prepare a typed list, arranged alphabetically, showing the holdings of the library, i.e. volumes and dates. This list is then posted where students and faculty may refer to it. Other libraries have a visible file which contains the checking cards which show the library holdings. This visible file, available from library supply houses or a stationer, may be a metal cabinet, a book form, or a rotary file.

Some libraries place a catalog card in the main catalog for each periodical received. The following rules apply if you decide to make a catalog card for periodicals:
1. Main entry is a title entry, using a hanging indentation.
2. Use an "open entry", that is, no closing date indicated if the periodical is still being published.
3. When a periodical stops publication, type or write the closing date on the catalog card.
4. If a periodical changes its name, make a card for the new name with a note below the record of holdings giving the former name. Close the entry on the former name and make a note referring to the new name.

Missionary broadcaster, v. 1-44
   Chicago, Scandinavian Alliance
   Mission; The Evangelical Alliance
   Mission, 1925-1968.

44 v. (7 issues a year)

Continued as Horizons

○

Horizons, v. 45-
   Chicago, The Evangelical Alliance
   Mission, 1969-

v. (7 issues a year)

Preceded by Missionary broadcaster

○

If the new title continues the numbering of volumes from its predecessor, it "continues" that publication. If the numbering of the new title begins with v.l, no. 1 as a completely new title, it "supersedes" the former publication and should be so indicated on the catalog card.

It is not necessary to indicate on the catalog card the holdings of the library for each periodical. A note may say "For information on holdings, consult library personnel."

Nonperiodical Serials

Serials not issued by a corporate body. All issues are cataloged on one set of cards giving only items of importance to all issues. Entry is under title with hanging indentation. Show frequency of issue, such as annual, biennial, etc. If the period covered by an annual publication is other than that of the calendar year, note the period, e.g., Report year ends June 30. The main entry card should show which volumes the library has, written in pencil or as a note referring to the shelf list. The shelf-list card should have a complete list of issues held by the library.

```
        Books for children.   1960/65-
          Chicago, American Library Association.

          v. annual

          Period covered by each vol. ends Aug. 31.
          Vols. for 1960/65- selected and reviewed
          by the Booklist and Subscription Books
          Bulletin.


                          ◯
```

```
The world almanac.   New York, World-
    Telegram.

       v. annual

Library has

1950-58
1964-
```

```
The world almanac.   New York, World-
    Telegram.

       v. annual

4382   1950
7659   1951
9873   1952 etc.



Shelf-list card
```

Serials issued by a corporate body. Make the main entry under title with an added entry under the corporate body. If the title includes the name of the corporate body or if the title is a general term, such as Memoirs, Studies, Annual Report, which needs the name of the body for identification, enter under the name of the corporate body.

```
252.08
M817    Moody Bible Institute.
            Founder's week messages.  Chicago, Moody
        Bible Institute, 1907-

        v.

        Library has 1959-62, 1967, 1970-

        1. Sermons.  I. Title.

                        ◯
```

When the main entry is under title, make an added entry card for the sponsoring corporate body. When the main entry is under the name of the corporate body, make an added entry title card. The shelf-list card should show the complete holdings of the library.

Monographic series. These may be cataloged in two ways. Each issue may be considered as an individual volume and cataloged like a book with the author as main entry, making an added entry for the series. If you prefer, you may enter under the title of the series, with hanging indentation and open entry. If you enter under series, make a contents note on the main entry card listing the titles and authors of all the volumes held by the library. Make the necessary analytic cards for each volume: author, title and subject. Make a shelf-list card noting volumes as added.

If a monographic series is cataloged as a series, the classification number will be the same for all volumes. Analytic cards for individual volumes should include the volume number as part of the call number since analytic cards refer to individual volumes. If each issue of a monographic series is cataloged separately, place it in the classification number which indicates the subject content of that specific title.

Microforms

Microfilms and microfiche are the most practical microforms for smaller libraries. Microfilm on reels was one of the first microforms and was used primarily for the preservation of material which was bulky and difficult to store, such as newspapers. It is now used to replace books and magazines as well, but in a small library because of the cost of reading machines and other factors, it is not used a great deal.

Students, especially in elementary and high school, enjoy learning to use the machines, and since use in higher education has become almost commonplace, it is good training for them. Usually back issues of periodicals and perhaps one newspaper are the most common holdings on the elementary and secondary level. Serials are available on 16mm and 35mm microfilm.

Microfiche is gaining in popularity. A microfiche "is a sheet of film containing multiple microimages in a grid pattern" or "the frames of a micro-film in sheet form." Many pages of print may be stored on one small sheet or card, usually 3"x5" or 4"x 6"

Microform readers, along with a brief discussion of machines for playing tapes and records will be discussed later in this section. A helpful, inexpensive ($1.00) manual which contains illustrations of microforms and their readers is available from the National Microfilm Association, Suite 1101, 8728 Colesville Road, Silver Springs, Maryland 20910, U.S.A. Ask for their *Introduction to Micrographics*. This does not discuss library procedures for organizing microforms, but it does have a helpful glossary and a bibliography of inexpensive booklets on the subject.

Because some seminary libraries may want to obtain and process microforms, a brief discussion of library procedures follows.

Cataloging and classification. The cataloging procedure for microforms is identical to that of its original form; in other words, if the original was a book, catalog the microform as a book or if the original was a periodical, catalog the microform as a periodical. The fact that it is in microform can be included in a note stating that it is a microfilm or microfiche. Some libraries simply type or stamp microfilm or microfiche at the head of the call number and otherwise catalog it as if it were in the original.

Care and storage. Microfilms should be stored in dustproof containers. They usually come on a plastic or metal reel and are provided with a paper tape upon which the name of the periodical or book and its identifying volume, dates, etc., can be written. The boxes in which the reels are enclosed can be used for writing the call number and the ownership marks. It is unnecessary to equip these for circulation since they must be used in the building. The boxes can be stored in special steel file cabinets made for this purpose, or they may be stored on shallow shelves. Film should not be stored in direct sunlight or near direct sources of heat. Temperature changes of more than 20 degrees F. are undesirable; a constant temperature of 70 degrees is ideal, but film can be used even if it must be stored in a building in which the temperature fluctuates from 60 to 90 degrees. Extremely humid or dry conditions should be avoided; fifty percent humidity is ideal. Reels of film should be fastened at the end with masking tape; rubber bands should not be used nor should fasteners nor containers which are composed of materials containing acid, sulphur, or peroxide. Some rubber bands which have been manufactured without sulphur are safe to use.

OPAQUE GRAPHIC AND PHOTOGRAPHIC MATERIALS

Flat Pictures

Visual material is always helpful and even a very small library with a limited budget can organize a picture file. Types of materials used are flat pictures, maps, charts and flashcards. This discussion is devoted primarily to flat pictures.

Before you begin to collect pictures the purpose of the collection should be clearly stated.
1. Is it to be used for teaching aids in a secular classroom, in a school for missionary children, or in a school for nationals?
2. Is it to be used for teaching aids for Christian education (Sunday school, Bible clubs, etc.) in a school for missionary children or nationals?
3. Is it to be used for young children, older children, college age, adults or for all ages?

There are many sources of visual materials. Free or inexpensive pictures may be obtained from magazines, calendars, book jackets, seed and nursery catalogs, old Sunday school literature, travel and advertising brochures, discarded illustrated books which are too worn to use but with salvagable illustrated material, children's coloring books, advertisements from business firms, "remainders" from Christian publishers (outdated picture rolls or picture sets from curricula no longer published or being listed in catalog).

Many religious publishers sell pictures related to Bible stories and Bible characters. These may be purchased when you order books.

Selection and processing. Not all colorful magazine pictures are suitable for inclusion in a picture file. The most important criterion for selection is that the picture will meet the needs of the users. Almost any picture on a subject may be kept if it is needed and the library has only a few, but as the collection grows, one can become more discriminating. Color is better than black and white but black and white is better than nothing. Consider also clarity and authenticity over aesthetic or artistic standards except for art reproductions. Some pictures may not be suitable for mounting but may be used on small cards with memory verses, or for making charts or illustrated maps.

Divide pictures desired for immediate use from those (including duplicates) which may be stored for future use. The latter need not be trimmed and can be filed roughly by subject or placed in a flat box. The former may be trimmed with a paper cutter or razor blade and ruler. Scissors are difficult to use because it is hard to cut a straight line with them.

After trimming, the pictures can be placed in folders or envelopes, but mounting is preferred for the better ones. Choose a good grade of paper because the wear on a picture file is great, and the mounting may become worn before the picture is. Mounting also protects the picture, makes it easier to use, and adds to its attractiveness and effectiveness. It is wise to use only one kind and size of mounting paper. If there is a paper processor near you, seek his advice; often you can make better arrangements with a local firm than with a national supplier. Some libraries use manila, tag, poster board, or construction paper. Be sure to use a mounting paper that is substantial enough to protect the pictures but not so heavy or bulky that it will take up too much space in the files.

Most librarians like to use a variety of colors for mounting. If this is possible, choose the color which compliments the coloring in the picture. Choice of adhesive varies with availability. It is wise to avoid starch-based paste because it is subject to insect damage. Some libraries use rubber cement because it is easy to clean off, and it does not cause the picture to wrinkle. It may eventually become dry and discolor, especially in an arid climate, but it has been used with some success by many librarians. Plastic adhesives, such as Elmer's "Glue-all" or Gaylord's "Magic-mend" are frequently recommended. Be sure to use enough adhesive so that pictures will bond to the mounting. Some librarians recommend tipping pictures with paste or glue at the four corners only, but this attachment is usually not strong enough to protect the pictures from wear. It leaves the edges loose so they are easily snagged or torn. The best way to mount a picture is to see that it is attached firmly and fully on all four sides. It is usually best to place only one picture on a mount, but one can save mounting paper by grouping two or three small pictures pertaining to the same subject on one mount.

The bottom margin should be slightly wider than the top. Center the picture on the mount so side margins are even. After finding the place for the picture on the mount, make light corner marks on the mount so there is a guide to aid in gluing the picture down after adhesive has been applied. After mounting, put sheets of waxed paper between the pictures and place a weight on them so they will not warp.

Subject headings. Information which is available with the picture should be saved and put with it. This helps in assigning subject headings to the pictures. Some libraries glue some textual information on the mounting paper. Usually this is all the information that is used, but some librarians do more research and add to the information. For art reproductions, it is essential to have the name of the artist and the title of his work; it is desirable to include the life dates of the artists. Write or type all information on a good grade of paper. If the information is lengthy, fasten it to the back of the mounting paper. Only brief captions and titles should be placed on the front. The source and date of publication should be placed on the picture caption or on the subject label.

Many libraries place subject headings on the front of the mount, but others prefer the back. Since the subject heading is not an integral part of the picture, some librarians think that a subject heading on the front detracts from the picture and defaces the front of the mount. An advantage of having subjects on the front is that the picture can face the front of the filing drawer so it does not have to be removed when a user is searching. Write the subject heading in ink or type it on a gummed label and place it in the upper left-hand corner of the mount as it will stand in the file drawer. Some libraries prefer to print or type the headings in capital letters. If labels are used, do not put them on the exact edge, but leave a small margin.

For unmounted materials, write the subject with a pencil in the margin as near the upper left corner as possible.

Postcards, because of their format, must have the information placed on the back.

Specific subject headings are usually best for pictures, but some pictures can be logically grouped under broad headings. It is usually better to use specific headings such as "Automobiles" rather than "Motor vehicles." Use of the materials is an important factor. If the users want pictures of a specific thing, then grouped headings lose much of the material for them, but if users want material grouped together for use in a unit of study such as "communication", the grouped heading is better.

A list of subject headings which is now published in its sixth edition and used widely by libraries in the United States is *The Picture Collection: Subject Headings*. See the bibliography for full bibliographic information. This listing is a grouped listing rather than a specific one so be prepared to edit it for your local needs. It is useful for its cross-referencing, but if funds are limited and you have a small picture collection, use the subject heading list for the pamphlet file.

A subject index on cards should be maintained for the picture file. Some school libraries classify their pictures by the same classification system which they use for their books. Many of them also catalog the pictures and place cards in the card catalog with "P" or "Pi" or "Picture" at the head of the call number to indicate that the material is in picture form. Some use a different color card for pictures.

Filing. Use a file cabinet large enough to hold legal-sized folders or use large boxes or cartons. Pictures may be filed in subject folders prepared as for pamphlets. Large pictures may be filed flat in large cardboard cartons or fastened by spring clothespins or clips to a wire strung along the wall. Some libraries mount large pictures on heavy kraft paper (procurable in rolls). Cut a piece of this paper ¼ inch smaller around than the picture to be mounted. Lay together with edges matching and bind around with masking tape.

Circulation. The same card that is used for other vertical file material may be used for pictures. Most libraries simply record the subject of the picture, identify it as pictures, record the number of pictures and have the user sign his name. The date due is stamped or written on the card. Pictures are then placed in a large envelope which is stamped with the date due, followed by borrower's name or the subject of the pictures and the number of pictures.

Some libraries prefer to use a different card for pictures and pamphlet material. A simple form follows:

```
No. of Pictures _____
Borrower       _____
Date Due       _____
Subject        _____
```

This information can be stamped or written on a plain card. Cards for pictures may be placed in the front of the circulation file of cards for books. When circulation is counted, the cards may be filed under date due. Usually these are filed behind the cards for books, under the heading "pictures." Upon return, the pictures should be counted and the card discarded or if a stamped or printed form is used, the name should be marked through and the card can be placed in a box for reuse. If the pictures are too large to circulate in envelopes, they can be rolled and wrapped in old newspaper or inserted in used mailing tubes.

A picture file is not an expensive part of a library's collection, but it can be very valuable to supplement classroom teaching. All libraries should maintain some type of file even if time and money is limited. Creative ideas for handling pictures may be suggested by a student aid and much of the work can be done by someone with little or no special training.

Maps

There are many forms of maps which represent subject or geographic areas. To form a call number for a map, use the letter M and the number of the map, such as M14 for the fourteenth map you add, or you may classify it by area, such as M940 for maps of Europe. If you have a separate file cabinet or drawer for maps, you may arrange them by the area covered.

If you do this, it is not necessary to catalog them. Write the area heading on the folded map or on a label on the map, in the upper right-hand corner. Arrange the maps alphabetically by: 1) continent; 2) country; 3) state, province; 4) county; 5) city or town such as:

Africa. Zambia. Lusaka.

North America. United States. Tennessee. Hamilton. Chattanooga.

If you prefer to file them in your pamphlet file, give each map a subject heading of the area covered, place it in a folder and file alphabetically.

Larger and more important maps should be cataloged with a card placed in the catalog. Give the following information for each map:

1. Location symbol (M14 or M940. Use the word MAP above the call number)
2. The area in capital letters
3. Title of map
4. Publisher or issuing body
5. Date
6. Series, if part of one
7. Size
8. Scale

Make an identical card for the shelf list in order to have a list of the maps in the library. File in a separate section of the shelf list.

```
Map
M14      MARYLAND, VIRGINIA, DELAWARE, WEST VIRGINIA
              The Mid-Atlantic states. National Geo-
         graphic Society. 1976. (Close-up: U.S.A.)
         col. map 22 X 34 in. fold. to 5-5/8 X
         8-3/4 in.

         Scale 1 inch to 14 miles
```

Charts, Posters and Graphs

Charts and graphs small enough to fit in the file drawer can be prepared for use and treated like pamphlets. Those that are larger can be mounted on cloth, rolled and stored in mailing tubes or they can be filed flat in large cartons or hung from a wire as large pictures are. Posters can also be treated as pictures or filed with pamphlets.

TRANSPARENT GRAPHIC AND PHOTOGRAPHIC MATERIALS

Slides

Slides are usually kept in groups by subject in special slide boxes or trays. They may be assigned a classification number and be cataloged like records and tapes except they are identified by "Slides" or "SL" above the call number. If you do not want to assign a classification number to slides, give them an accession number, such as SL24 for the twenty-fourth set of slides added to the library.

The title is used for the main entry of a slide followed by the word (Slide) in parentheses. Using a hanging indentation, give the publisher or source, if known, date, if known. In the collation include the number of slides, if a set; size of the slides; and whether black and white or in color. Make added entries for subjects as for books, if you wish. Make a shelf-list card for each set of slides, to be filed in a separate section of the shelf list.

```
SL
2          Impressionist painting (Slide), by Albert
           Chatelet.  New York, McGraw-Hill, 1962.
           24 2 X 2 in. slides.  col.

           Book guide.

             1. Impressionism (Art)   2. Painting.
           3. Art.
```

Filmstrips

Assign a number to each filmstrip added to the library. This number preceded by FS is the call number, e.g., FS8 is the call number for the eighth filmstrip added to the library. Place the call number on the container for the filmstrip and on the catalog and shelf-list cards.

The main entry of a filmstrip is under the title followed by the word (Filmstrip) in parentheses. The title is usually found on the title frame. Using hanging indentation, include the name of the producer or the organization responsible for the filmstrip, and the date. The collation includes the number of frames, if numbered, or 1 reel; whether black and white or color; width in millimeters. If a recording accompanies the filmstrip, give a physical description: for phonodiscs, give number of sides, diameter in inches, playing speed in revolutions per minute: for phonotapes, give number of reels, diameter of reels in inches, speed if available. Include information about accompanying material such as a guide or teachers' manual. If part of an important series, include a series note in parentheses after the collation. A short summary of the contents will be valuable to the user. Use subject headings to make the filmstrip useful to your patrons.

```
FS
11        Geography of the holy land (Filmstrip)
              Family Filmstrips, 1959.
              51 fr. col. 35 mm. and phonodisc, 2 s.
          12 in. 33 1/3 rpm. With guide. (Understand-
          ing the Bible Lands)
              Summary:  Photographs show 4 natural geo-
          graphic sections of Palestine with distinct
          features and characteristics.

              1. Palestine - Description, geography.
              2. Geography - Pictorial works.  (Series)

                             O
```

Care must be observed in storing and handling films. Films should be kept in dustproof boxes and be cleaned and inspected after each use. Handle by the edges with care and be careful not to drop them. Avoid scratches, fingerprints, tears, twists and dampness. Film should be at room temperature before projecting.

Where practical, supply with cards and pockets, but a card similar to the one used for vertical file material can be used for the circulation record if preferred. Be sure that full identification is written on the circulation card.

Motion Pictures

Motion pictures are entered under title followed by the designation (Motion Picture) or (Film) in parentheses. If the title is lacking, the librarian should supply one. The sponsor or producer is given. If the releasing agent differs from the producer, that name is noted also. Date of release follows the name of releasing agent. If date is not known, use the copyright date. If neither date is known, use a probable date with a question mark, e.g., 1976? Collation includes running time, sd. for sound, si. for silent, col. for color, b&w for black and white, and width in millimeters, e.g., 16mm. Include notes for further information. A brief summary on the card is especially helpful to users.

Some libraries use accession numbers instead of a classification number for motion pictures as well as for other types of nonbook material. Whether a classification or accession number is used, be sure the film, the film case, as well as the catalog cards are numbered. Stamp ownership marks on the film case.

Films usually are checked out on a special card held at the circulation desk, but some libraries equip them with cards and pockets. Some use a sheet of paper for check out. Few libraries can afford to purchase films, and film rentals and returns can be time consuming. Often the person who takes care of the projectors is also charged with the responsibility of taking care of rentals.

```
F
6          God's word in man's language (Film)
           New York, American Bible Society, 1954.
           25 min.  sd.  col.  16 mm.

           Summary:  Dr. Eugene Nida explains
           difficulty of translating Bible into
           various languages.

             1. Bible - Translating.  2. Language and
           languages.

                              O
```

Transparencies

A transparency is an image produced on transparent material and is used with an overhead projector. Transparencies are entered under title, followed by the word (Transparency) in parentheses. If a title is not given, the cataloger must supply one. The collation includes the number of pieces and the size of the transparency. A transparency with overlays is considered one piece. Notes are added to explain collation or indicate use. Transparencies may be assigned subject headings and filed in flat folders with other flat material.

THREE DIMENSIONAL MATERIALS

Many libraries acquire, organize and circulate material which is nonprint media. Material which is useful as instructional aids has a legitimate place in a library. To what extent a library chooses to stock nonprint material is largely dependent on budget, staff and demand. If budget and staff are adequate, some of the manuals and books listed in the bibliography should be purchased so that the person in charge of the library will have more comprehensive instruction for acquiring and organizing material.

Any type of material which can be correlated with instruction and the library has room to store is good to have. Globes, models, specimens, crafts, kits, etc. are all helpful. Some schools assign these to classrooms rather than keep them in the library. Cabinets or open shelves can be used for storing these materials and some kind of record should be available to the user.

This can be a list of materials, but major items may be classified and cataloged with an identifying heading above the call number and the type of material in parentheses following the title. Some libraries prefer to catalog all types of materials except pictures. Many put all small materials into the vertical file and catalog only those which are too large to fit. Inexpensive ephemeral material should not be cataloged. The procedures for cataloging are similar to those used for other types of nonbook materials.

Models, Dioramas, Realia

Models include globes, relief models and other items. If a library has only one globe, it is not necessary to catalog it, but if a library chooses to record everything it has, enter it under the area in capital letters as if it were a subject entry. Follow with the title at second indentation followed by the word (Globe) or (Celestial globe). Include publisher or issuing body, date, size (in diameter) and the scale. A note should state the material of which the globe is made, such as glass, plastic, rubber.

Models are entered under title, followed by the word (Model). Collation includes the number of pieces or the size. Other explanatory material can be given in a note.

Dioramas are scenes produced in three dimensions against an appropriate background.

Realia is used to designate specific objects or specimens such as rocks, stuffed birds, sea shells, etc. Enter both dioramas and realia under title followed by the appropriate designation in parentheses.

All other types of similar materials are entered under title. Use any other kind of information which seems important to identify the material. Where practical, supply with cards and pockets, but a card similar to the one used for pamphlet file material can be used for the circulation record if preferred. Be sure that full identification is written on the circulation card.

SOUND REPRODUCTIONS

Recordings and tapes (reel and cassette) are relatively easy to process and contribute a great deal to teaching and learning. A practical consideration is whether the library or its patrons provide the equipment necessary to play the recordings and tapes. Many libraries acquire and catalog the materials and circulate them, but they make no attempt to furnish the machines. Others stock the materials with the understanding that the institution will buy and make available the machines, at least for use by instructors. Some libraries have one tape player and one record player which can be used in the library, usually with ear phones, but they make no provision for groups to use the materials in the library. Frequently the machines are borrowed by the faculty for classroom use.

Records and tapes are being produced which are useful in various areas of knowledge, but probably the first ones to be acquired should be in the area of music. So varied is the choice that no realistic advice could be given other than that selection should be done with the curricular and recreational needs of the library users in mind. Sources for records and tapes are suggested in the bibliography.

Cataloging and classification. Some libraries assign a Dewey Decimal classification number to records and tapes as they do to books. Other libraries do not classify records and tapes, but use an accession number, such as Rec 9 for the ninth record added to the library. An identification term or symbol is used as part of the call number, such as "Record" or "Rec" for phonograph records; "RA" for record albums; "Tape" or "RT" for reel tapes and "CT" for tapes in cassettes. Identification of the type of material follows the title on the catalog cards, using the singular form of the descriptive word in parentheses, e.g., (Phonodisc) for phonograph records; (Reel, Tape); (Cassette, Tape). Some libraries prefer to use a different color of card for sound materials in order to help the user spot them quickly in the card catalog.

The cataloging of musical records and tapes can be very detailed if complete information is given on the catalog card. This is not necessary, however, for small libraries. Using the information on the record label or tape container, make the composer the main entry. The title is followed by the appropriate descriptive word in parentheses, as (Phonodisc). The imprint consists of the manufacturer's or publisher's name and the serial identification (album or record number); give the serial number of a tape, if available; if not, give the date of issue. The collation for records includes the number of sides, size, speed and "stereo" if the recording is stereophonic rather than monaural; for tapes, include the type of tape (reel or cassette), speed for reel, playing time and "stereo", if applicable. In a note, include the name of the performer, the instrument and the title on the reverse side of the disc. If there are more than two works on a record or tape, a contents note may be added. If there are several separate works by many composers, or if there is no composer (as folk music), the main entry is under title, using hanging indentation. Separate cataloging is done for each work on a record, in an album or on a tape. Added entries may be made for subject (the musical form, such as Symphony or Hymns) and performer. Make a shelf-list card like the main entry card through the collation; add the source, date and cost on the second line below the collation. File shelf-list cards for records and tapes separate from the cards for books.

If there are booklets or other materials, such as libretto, which accompany the recording, it is best to keep them with the recording. Such material may be put in a pocket which is fastened or pasted to the record holder, tape container or album case or slipped into the album case. A note should be put on the catalog card such as "Libretto in pocket" or "Historical information in pocket." If the material is too bulky, you may put it in the vertical file under the appropriate subject. If this is done, a note should be added to the card, e.g., "Libretto in vertical file under MUSIC."

Catalog nonmusical records and tapes under author. If there is no author, or if there are many authors, use the title as main entry. Sir Cedric Hardwicke's reading of Wordsworth's poetry is entered under Wordsworth. A poet reading his own poetry is entered under his name, but if the poet read from several poets, the entry would be under title. Catalog sermons or speeches using the preacher or speaker as main entry. If a tape is one of an important series, include the name of the series in parentheses following the collation.

For small collections, avoid an elaborate and time-consuming system of cataloging and processing. Many collections that start small, however, soon grow large enough that some system is required so that users can locate materials quickly and easily.

Examples:

MAIN ENTRY CARD
RECORD ALBUM

```
RA
8       Handel, George Frederick, 1685-1759.
          Messiah (Record album)  RCA S2RS-4245.
          6 s.  12 in.  33 1/3 rpm.  stereo.

          Sir Malcolm Sargent, Conductor, Royal
        Philharmonic Orchestra.
          Notes and libretto in album case.

          1. Oratorios.  I. Title.
```

SHELF-LIST CARD

```
RA
8       Handel, George Frederick, 1685-1759.
          Messiah (Record album)  RCA S2RS-4245.
          6 s.  12 in.  33 1/3 rpm.  stereo.

          Fellowship Book Store   11/4/73   $12.48
```

ADDED ENTRY - TITLE CARD

```
RA        Messiah
8         Handel, George Frederick
```

ADDED ENTRY - SUBJECT CARD

```
RA        ORATORIOS
8         Handel, George Frederick, 1685-1759.
            Messiah (Record album) RCA S2RS-4245
```

MAIN ENTRY CARD
CASSETTE, TAPE

```
CT
35        Smith, Wilbur Moorehead
            He's coming again (Cassette, Tape)
          Released by G/L Publications, 1971.
            Cassette. 31 min. (The end times)

            Side 2: The master of deception.

            1. Eschatology.  2. Second advent.
          I. Title. (Series)
```

Circulation and storage. Write the call number on the jacket or record holder or on the box containing the tape. Pockets and cards are typed for record or album. Be sure that the card has a notation indicating pieces, e.g., "6 records and miniature score", so that the person receiving the material at the circulation desk can check at once to see that all material is returned. Note of any damage or missing items should be made on the card when the material is returned, e.g., side 2 of record is scratched; booklet missing; record 3 missing.

Records should be shelved upright on the shelves to prevent warping. Special record shelves or holders are available. Few libraries attempt to shelve records with books. Tapes are usually also shelved in a separate place from books; often they are placed in tape boxes and shelved with the records. Cassettes can be placed in special holders which resemble books and shelved with the books, or they may be placed in small boxes and shelved with reel tapes and records. Be sure that the call numbers are on the boxes and that the pockets and cards are attached for easy identification and circulation. Ownership marks should always be stamped or written on all of these materials. Some libraries stamp the label or seal on the record as well as on the record holder; some use the name of the library on the pocket and card as the ownership mark.

EQUIPMENT

There is such a wide variety of machines offered on the market to use with sound and transparent materials, that it is impossible to discuss them in a brief treatment. Power conditions vary widely also, so that in some cases only battery operated equipment is possible.

Record players, tape and cassette players are relatively inexpensive and would probably be practical for the library to purchase and make available to its users. Consult local firms for prices and types.

Microfilm readers and reader printers are more expensive. If local firms do not have information on them, write for the free booklet: *Buyer's Guide to Microfilm Equipment* published by the National Microfilm Association.

Slide projectors, motion picture projectors and overhead projectors vary widely in cost.

A comprehensive guide for all of this equipment may be ordered from the National Audio-Visual Association, Fairfax, Virginia 05454, U.S.A. Ask for the latest edition of their annual *Audio-Visual Equipment Directory*.

11. CARE AND PRESERVATION OF LIBRARY MATERIALS

Since the materials in your collection are valuable and you want to be prudent in the use of your library budget, careful attention must be given to the condition and maintenance of library materials.

THE CARE OF BOOKS

Opening Books
Much damage may be done to a book by careless or ignorant handling when opening it. If you and your staff make it a consistent practice to open books correctly, you may prolong the life of your books. Place the book on a table or other flat surface with the spine down and the fore edges up. Gently, but firmly, press down the front cover, then the back cover where they join the body of the book. Open a few pages next to the front and the back alternately, pressing firmly but gently along the inner margins of the pages, thus decreasing the possibility of breaking the binding. Continue opening and pressing a few pages at a time until you reach the center of the book. Paperbound books are particularly susceptible to breaking of the binding since many of them have pages and covers which are glued instead of sewn.

Collating
In order to make certain that a book is complete and perfect, turn the pages one by one to check that all are there, that the pages are in correct order and that there are no omissions nor imperfections. Check to see if the cover is damaged, if the corners are bent or broken, if the lining is loose. Return damaged or imperfect books to the bookseller or the publisher. With a letter knife, separate pages that have not been cut apart.

Marking Ownership
In order to mark books easily, buy a rubber stamp with the name and address of the library. DO NOT disfigure the title page with your ownership mark or other notations. The ownership mark may be stamped on the bottom edges of the book pages while the pages are held together tightly. The book pocket also should be stamped with the ownership mark. Formerly many libraries used a "secret page" (the same page number for all books) on which to stamp the ownership mark, on the assumption that such a mark would prevent theft or would assist in identifying library property. Generally, this practice has been discontinued.

Some librarians use the first right-hand page following the title page to pencil near the left margin the following notations: source, cost, date of accession, call number. The accession number is written in ink one inch from the top or the bottom of the same page. It is not necessary to note in the book the source, cost and date of accession if you use an accession book or if you place the information on the shelf-list card.

Shelf Life of Books

Most libraries store books vertically on wooden or metal shelves. It is necessary that book supports be used, for if shelves are too full, damage by rubbing and friction may result when books are pushed in or removed. A book may also be easily damaged by pulling if from the shelf by the top of its spine, weakening or tearing the binding. Space on the shelves should be flexible so that a book may be held firmly by its spine to remove it from the shelf. If, however, the shelf is not full enough, the books may lean or sag, warping the book and pulling the pages from the spine. To remedy this, purchase commercial supports to suspend from the bottom of the metal shelf above or metal bookends which stand on the shelf. A clay brick covered with cloth or thick paper also makes an adequate book support.

The type of bookmark used by your patrons may be of concern to you, for many people have a habit of turning down a corner of a page to mark where they ceased reading, thereby weakening the paper and causing the corner to tear off later. An assistant may make attractive bookmarks to be given away by the library as a reminder to patrons not to deface or mark a page in a book. You may also find it necessary to remind students not to write in books, bend the spines back, or put things in books which cause stress against the hinges or stitching.

Dusting

Books should be kept clean. If the collection is small, frequent use of the books will prevent dust from collecting on them. Some books will be used rarely, however, and a regular schedule should therefore be set for dusting shelves and books. A vacuum cleaner with a hose connection and a brush of soft bristles on the end is a good method of dusting if care is taken that loose bindings and pages are not damaged. A soft, dry cloth is satisfactory for dusting if the cloth is washed frequently and if it is not used to grind dust into the books. Start dusting at the top shelf so that any dust which falls to a lower shelf may be removed as you progress to the bottom shelf.

PREVENTING DAMAGE

Humidity

Excessive humidity causes mold and mildew, the loosening of paste and glue and the weakening of paper and leather. Mold is a downy or furry growth, caused by fungi, and forms on book covers or inside a book. Mildew also is caused by fungi, resulting in a thin, furry, whitish coating and discoloration.

Humidity may be decreased or removed by artificial heat, such as light bulbs. Some wooden bookcases are constructed with an outlet for a light bulb. Be sure to leave air space around the bulb and use a wire protector for the bulb, if possible. The increased circulation of dry air by means of fans helps to prevent mold. Electrically operated dehumidifiers are very effective in decreasing humidity.

Dryness

Central heating is harmful to books, for dry heat takes the life out of paper and leather. Various devices may be purchased for attachment to radiators, then filled with water which increases the humidity by evaporation. In hot, dry climates some librarians place receptacles of water near the bookshelves, thus adding moisture to the air by evaporation. Green plants or flowers which must be watered frequently make an attractive method of adding moisture as the water in the plant container evaporates. Electric humidifiers also are available. An average humidity of 50 to 60 percent is desirable. Use of a hygrometer to measure humidity is essential unless the library is air conditioned or unless the humidifier or dehumidifier has humidistatic control.

Insect Pests

In addition to damage to books from dampness or dryness, much destruction may result from insects. The following recommendations for the treatment of insects are based on the books by Jannette Newhall and Harry Lydenberg cited in the bibliography.

The prevention of harm by insects is much preferred to the destruction of insects after they have appeared. The maintenance of correct limits of heat and humidity, along with high standards of housekeeping help to avert damage. Chemicals which by their odor repel insects, are preferable to those which kill after books have been damaged. Some insects, however, build up an immunity to insecticides. Books should not be sprayed with an insecticide, but walls, shelves and dark corners should be sprayed periodically, more often in tropical than in temperate zones.

Bookworms. Bookworms, which are seldom found in temperate climates, usually make their homes in tropical and semitropical climates. The damage from bookworms occurs from the larvae of a large variety of beetles which lay their eggs on the spines or edges of books. After hatching, the larvae eat their way into the book, feeding on the paste and glue. Soon the larvae develop into beetles and repeat the cycle, sometimes completely perforating a book so that it cannot be repaired.

A library which is widely infected by bookworms should be fumigated professionally. Fumigation should be repeated after a few days to kill any remaining larvae. If only a few books are infected, they may be placed in an airtight container with a suitable fumigant. The fumigant will give off fumes which will kill most insects if the books or other materials are arranged to allow for circulation of the fumes. The material should stay in the container for the length of time required by the specific fumigant. After removal, the material should be set aside for a time and inspected for larvae before being returned to the shelves. The fumigant or insecticides used should be the safest ones for human beings. If you have no one in your school to advise you, the local department of health or agriculture may be able to advise you about the best insecticides to use for different purposes.

Any book which has a sign of bookworms should be removed from the shelf and segregated until it can be treated. An extremely damaged book should be burned and replaced by a new copy if possible.

Cockroaches and silverfish. The cockroach is a straight-winged, crawling insect with a flat, yellowish-brown or black body, slender legs, and long feelers. The silverfish is a wingless insect with silvery scales, long feelers and a bristly tail. These insects thrive in dampness and darkness and are attracted by glue and paste.

To prevent damage from them, walls, wooden book shelves and dark corners should be sprayed periodically with an insecticide. Silverfish may be destroyed by spreading a mixture of boric acid and flour where they may encounter it. One library has used jelly glasses placed at frequent intervals, with masking tape or other adhesive in strips up the outside of each glass and a teaspoon of flour inside each glass. The siverfish climb into the glass to reach the flour, are trapped inside, and are unable to crawl out.

Termites. Termite is the name of an order of insects that live in communities in soil, damp wood or dry wood. About 1200 different species are known. Some termites build huge mounds of soil as high as twenty feet. Others nest underground, extending their burrows into wooden structures. They eat wood, paper and other materials which contain cellulose, the main ingredient of paper. They do much damage in their effort to find food as they tunnel their way through the woodwork of buildings, destroying books and furniture.

The best prevention against termites is an architectural precaution of providing a building which has no wooden surfaces in contact with soil. If termites are noticed, an insecticide should be used to spray all cracks in floors and wooden walls. If a building is greatly infested by termites, it may be necessary to employ an exterminator to destroy them.

12. PLANNING A LIBRARY BUILDING

The need to plan a library building is a tremendous responsibility. It should be undertaken with a full awareness of the complexity of a library's operation. The various functions must be properly interrelated with adequate space allowed for each function's services, personnel, resources, furniture and equipment. Future growth must be projected and provision made for expansion of the facility as growth demands.

The facility should be located centrally as tacit testimony to the role the library is expected to play in the school's teaching program. Objectives of the school and of the library need to be clearly stated as a guide in the development of the building plans. It makes a difference whether the library is viewed as a storehouse for books, or whether it is viewed as a vital part of the teaching program in which there is constant interaction of users with the resources — research, wide reading, exploration of ideas, etc. Provision for the use of nonbook media has a bearing on the design—are these integrated with printed materials or housed separately? Provision must be made for storage and use of hardware (projectors, audio equipment, microprint readers) and its maintenance.

Much literature is available to aid in building planning, and it is not the purpose of this chapter to give an exhaustive study of the laborious process that is involved. Sources listed in the bibliography give a wealth of data to aid inexperienced persons. What follows are some procedures or steps in the planning process and in the implementation of those plans. These are written out of personal experience with a prayer that they may throw light on the path of someone who may feel bewildered at the prospect of preparing for a new library facility.

First read, widely and thoughtfully, literature on the subject. This may mean sending for it overseas; therefore, long-range planning is indicated. Develop a notebook of ideas that come through this reading adventure. For some there may be no opportunity to visit other library buildings, but if this should be possible, much can be learned from observation and interviewing personnnel working in these libraries. Jot down their comments, both negative and positive.

Second, develop a clear statement of objectives for the library in terms of resources to be provided (books, periodicals, newspapers, pamphlets and clippings, pictures, microforms, recordings, slides, films, filmstrips and other nonbook media) and services (technical processes, circulation, reserve books, reference, bibliographic instruction).

Third, prepare a "program" for the library building. A program is a carefully prepared written statement to guide the architect in the building design. It describes the library's functions and their interrelationships (e.g., card catalog close to staff work area and accessible to circulation and the public), as well as the philosophy underlying the library's services to the academic community. It gives an estimate of future growth. Perhaps a few questions might be helpful here: How many resources does the library have, what kind (see objectives above), and what rate of increase is anticipated? How many students and faculty are to be served? What is the level of the student population--

undergraduate, graduate, Bible school, seminary? Do the faculty need research resources and facilities? Will the library need to serve as study hall or do students have other study facilities to use when they do not need access to library resources?

For a fuller statement about the program see the bibliography for information for obtaining a copy of "Some Notes on the Preparation of a Library Building."

Fourth, work closely with the architect as he/she prepares the building plans based on the program submitted to him. This program must be carefully reviewed and approved by the Administration of the school and its building committee.

The architect submits preliminary plans for review by his/her clients. These plans must be given thorough scrutiny in the light of the program. It is important to **take time** to deliberate! A keen imagination, an analytical mind, a ruler and notebook are invaluable at this stage. If you cannot read the blueprints, you must learn to do so, including the mechanical and electrical drawings when they are submitted later on. For example, be sure that light switches and electrical outlets are conveniently located and will not be covered by furniture or equipment.

In this preliminary stage, changes can be made quite easily. Do not allow pressure to hurry the plans to the point of "no return." Once the plans have been accepted and submitted, changes in the mechanical and electrical design are usually very costly. Also, complications develop when the changes were not coordinated with all the features involved; e.g., changing wall locations affects the heating and electrical installations.

Fifth, the planning of the interior layout of the building should be coordinated with the building design. This is important so that the proper space allocations will be made for placement of bookshelves, tables and chairs for library users and work stations for staff members. The furniture must be so placed that there is space for traffic flow when users occupy the chairs. Normally this requires four or five feet between tables and between tables and shelves.

The following dimensions for bookshelves, tables and chairs may be helpful to you, not only in planning a new building, but also in remodeling or rearranging an established library. Bookshelves or stacks are usually 3 feet (or I meter) in width for each section, with two or three or more sections joined together. Each shelf of a section is 8" (20cm) or 10" (25cm) deep. The number of shelves to a section depends upon the height of a section. High stacks (82") used for most of the book collection have seven shelves. Medium-height stacks (50"), sometimes used as room dividers, have four shelves. Counter height stacks (39") have three shelves. Double-face shelves, often called "free standing", permit books to be stored on both sides. Do not use a single-face stack except against a wall. The stack should be fastened by screws or braces to the wall, for high stacks can tip over unless securely placed.

To determine the number of stacks you will need, estimate storing 20 volumes per shelf. A 36" shelf will hold about 30 volumes, but by estimating 20 volumes for each shelf, you will leave room for growth of your collection. A new employee on your staff may not realize that books are shelved from left to right on the top shelf of a 3' section, then left to right on the second shelf, proceeding to the bottom of one section, then starting next with the top shelf of the second section, etc., going from left to right down the row of sections or around the room, however your stacks are placed. The aisle between stacks should be no less than 36" or l meter in order to permit books to be shelved easily and to allow for easy access by more than one person.

Tables and chairs for libraries are usually made of wood, but other materials prove satisfactory if furniture of high quality is obtained. For comfortable study at tables, the space per person should be no less than 30"x20" (76 cm x 51 cm). A table 90"x40" (2.28 m x 1.01 m) could seat six people. Avoid seating more than six people at a table, if possible. Chairs should be well made, with the seat height not less than 10" (25 cm) below the height of the tables. Armchairs require more space than straight chairs. Try to provide seating for half of the student enrollment at one time. More seating may be required if students must use the library as a study hall.

Colors chosen for walls, draperies affect the general atmosphere which is created. Ease of maintenance as well as economy should be important considerations; e.g., a brick wall does not need painting. Floor maintenance is crucial, but also consider the noise factor.

Flexibility is significant in a library building and is realized by the use of non-weight-bearing walls (between weight-bearing pillars). Large open areas can be divided into cozy study space with the use of free standing bookshelves.

Sixth, the plans as finally revised must be approved by the Administration, probably through the Building Committee.

Seventh, the Administration hires a contractor (or builder) by whatever route this is done in your locality--bids, direct negotiation, or other.

Eight, there must be adequate on-site supervision and a clear understanding as to who is reponsible--the architect, an associate architect, someone on the school's staff. Constant and careful vigilance is needed to see that plans are carefully followed.

Ninth, the arrangement with the contractor should provide for a certain period during which errors and defects in the building must be corrected—a warranty period.

The vision of a new building begins with the ideal as far as that can be expressed. However, when the plans are committed to paper, some compromises are inevitable and, in accordance with priorities adopted, some ideals have to be sacrificed. Careful planning will bring great dividends in the satisfaction that the inevitable shortcomings in any building are there, not by accident but by necessary accommodation.

Since it is difficult to keep all essentials in mind, this chapter concludes with a checklist to consider as you plan. Make your own checklist as you develop your plans and keep it before you, lest an important item be overlooked.

A checklist of items to consider in planning a library building:
1. Location—central, accessible, visible
2. Architecture—match existing style, or contrast
3. Atmosphere to be created within the building—formal or informal, warm, friendly, open
4. Functions to be performed—list them, e.g., technical processes, circulation, teaching, etc.

5. Interrelationships of functions, e.g., staff work area and card catalog, also public access to card catalog, etc.
6. Housing library resources—list by type, quantity, anticipated growth
7. Expandibility of building
8. Flexibility within the building (use nonweight-bearing walls, use book stacks for dividers, etc.)
9. Cost of administration—plan exits and traffic control for minimum staffing at low peak hours
10. Book return when library is closed
11. Adequate storage—e.g., gift books till they can be processed, etc.
12. Lighting—according to local standards, adjusted to various areas and needs
13. Heating and ventilation—air conditioning?
14. Moisture control to protect resources
15. Need a vault for rare or precious items?
16. Special storage space for projectors, record players, etc. to provide visual control, i.e., a place for each item
17. Space for custodial supplies and equipment
18. If more than one floor, a lift for book trucks
19. Rest room facilities
20. Staff lounge
21. A loading dock for delivery of cartons of books, etc.
22. Bulletin boards, display areas, but remember that exhibit space requires staff time
23. Pencil sharpeners

APPENDICES

I. DEFINITIONS

ACCESSION: To record books and other materials added to a library in the order in which they are received, giving a sequential number to each item.

ACCESSION BOOK: A book with numbered lines for recording information about books as they are received by the library.

ACCESSION NUMBER: The number given to a book in the order of its receipt. If an accession book is used, the accession number corresponds to the number of the line on which a condensed description of the book has been written.

ACQUISITION: Obtaining books and other materials by purchasing or by receiving as gifts.

ADDED ENTRY: Any catalog card for a book in addition to the main entry. For example, cards for titles, editors, series, joint authors.

ALPHABETIZING: Arranging cards according to the alphabet.

ALTERNATIVE TITLE: A second title introduced by "or" or its equivalent.

ANALYTIC: A catalog entry for a part of a book or work for which a comprehensive entry has been made. There are author, title, subject, series, author and title, and title and author analytics.

ANNOTATION: A brief description of the contents of a book, etc.

ANNUAL: A work published every year, such as annual report.

ANONYMOUS: Applied to a work published without indication of the author; of unknown authorship.

ANONYMOUS CLASSIC: A literary work whose authorship is lost in history, such as a folk epic, folk story.

AUTHOR: The person or corporate body responsible for the intellectual or artistic content of a work; the writer of a book.

AUTHOR ANALYTIC: A catalog entry identifying the author of a part of a book or other work.

AUTHOR AND TITLE ANALYTIC: Added entry for the author and title of a separate work which is part of a larger work, such as an anthology of several works each by a different author.

AUTHOR ENTRY: A card filed in the catalog under the name of the author of a book or other work, whether a main entry or an added entry.

AUTHOR NUMBER: Letters and numbers used to identify the author's family name, used in the call number of a book. See also CUTTER NUMBER.

AUTHOR STATEMENT: The author's name written with any joint authors.

AUTHORITY FILE: A record of "authoritative" forms of words for subject headings, form of the author's name or other terms as needed to keep entries in the catalog uniform. Use the same form every time.

BIBLIOGRAPHIC NOTE: A note on a catalog card which tells the user of the catalog that there is a bibliography in the work cataloged.

BIBLIOGRAPHY: A list of books, periodical articles an other works, usually giving order information including author, title, publisher and date.

BIOGRAPHER: The author of a work about another person or persons.

BIOGRAPHY: A book or work about the life of a person or persons.

BODY OF THE CARD: The part of the catalog card which begins with the title and ends with the imprint.

BOOK: A written or printed unit of library material which includes paper bound as well as cloth bound items.

BOOK CARD: A card for an individual book, used to keep circulation records.

BOOK CATALOG: A book containing catalog cards for library materials, arranged according to a definite plan. Some libraries use a book catalog instead of a card catalog.

BOOK JACKET: (or DUST JACKET): The loose paper covering, sometimes decorated, placed around a book.

BOOK NUMBER: The letters and numbers used to distinquish an individual book from all others having the same classification number. See also WORK NUMBER.

BOOK POCKET: A small, heavy envelope pasted in a book to hold the book card.

BOOK REQUEST FORM: A form in which patrons may record information about a book in order to have it considered for purchase by the library.

CALL NUMBER: A combination of letters and figures used to identify a particular book in the library. It includes the classification number and an author number, and may include a work number (work mark).

CARD CATALOG: A file of cards representing library materials.

CASSETTE: A small box to hold film or magnetic tape. Cassette tapes are enclosed in a sealed container, which fits into position on the recorder, eliminating the need for manual threading. The cassette is flipped over to play the second track or side.

CATALOG: A list of books, periodicals, etc. arranged according to a definite plan, representing the material in a specific collection. It may be either a card catalog or a book catalog.

CATALOGING: The preparation of cards to describe each particular book. It includes descriptive cataloging and subject cataloging.

CHARGING: Recording the loan of books or other library material borrowed for use outside the library.

CIRCULATION: The method of lending books and other library materials to borrowers and keeping records of the loans.

CLASS: A division of a classification system which is arranged by subject; a subject group; a subject number assigned to an item.

CLASSIFICATION: Arranging books by subject matter so that books on the same topic or field of knowledge stand together on the shelves. It includes assigning a number to a work according to its subject.

CLASSIFICATION SCHEDULE: The printed scheme of a particular classification system.

CLASSIFIED CATALOG: A catalog arranged by subject according to a classification scheme.

CLOSE CLASSIFICATION: Classifying books or other material in minute subdivisions of the subject.

CLOSED ENTRY: An entry for a serial publication, such as a periodical, which is no longer being published, or which the library no longer receives. See OPEN ENTRY.

COLLATE: To examine a book page by page to see that the printing, paging, binding are not defective.

COLLATION: The part of the catalog card which is the physical description of a work, giving such information as paging, number of volumes, illustrations.

COLLECTION: The entire group of materials in a library, such as books, periodicals and audio-visual materials.

COLLECTIVE TITLE: The title under which a group of books or other library materials is published. Each of these materials may also have its own individual title.

COMPILER: One who brings together the writing of several authors into a single book, or chooses and combines into one work selections or quotations from one author.

COMPOUND FAMILY NAME: A family name from two or more proper names, often connected by a hyphen, conjunction or preposition.

CONTENTS NOTE: A list of separate works or pieces included in a collective work.

CONTINUATION: A work issued as a supplement to one previously issued; a part issued in continuance of a book, a serial, or a series.

CONVENTIONAL TITLE: A title chosen as the best known of a work published under many different titles or forms. Also called FORM TITLE, UNIFORM TITLE.

COPY: One example of a book or other piece of library material; one object.

COPYRIGHT: The exclusive right granted by a government to publish a work during a stated number of years; a protection against others copying it.

COPYRIGHT DATE: The date the copyright is granted; usually found on the back of the title page.

CORPORATE BODY: A group of persons acting together as a unit, such as an association, church, or institution.

CORPORATE ENTRY: The name of a corporate body used as the catalog entry. It may be either the main entry or an added entry.

COVER TITLE: The title printed on the original covers of a book or pamphlet, or on the publisher's binding.

CROSS REFERENCE CARD: A card referring users of the catalog from one word or term to another.

CUTTER (verb): To assign a cutter number using the Cutter-Sanborn table.

CUTTER NUMBER: A letter plus the number taken from a system of notation devised by C. A. Cutter to identify the author of a work. The enlarged and revised volume by Kate E. Sanborn is known as the Cutter-Sanborn table.

DATE DUE SLIP: A paper form pasted in a library book on which is stamped the date the book should be returned to the library.

DATER: A rubber stamp for recording dates. Also called BAND DATER.

DESCRIPTIVE CATALOGING: Establishing the main entry and organizing the description of the physical book for entry on the catalog card.

DICTIONARY CATALOG: A catalog in which all the entries (author, title, subject, added entries) are arranged in alphabetical order.

DIGIT: A single numeral or figure, 1 to 9 and 0. The author number R38 is made up of the letter R and two digits, 3 and 8.

DIVIDED CATALOG: A catalog separated into two or more parts, usually author-title and subject.

DUST JACKET: See BOOK JACKET.

EDITION: All of the copies of a work printed at one time from the same plates or type; also, all the copies produced in the same form without revision. Each new edition implies changes or additions to the text.

EDITOR: A person who prepares someone else's work for publication.

END PAPER: The paper which lines the inside front and back covers of a book and also forms the flyleaves.

ENTRY: The name, word or phrase under which a card is filed in the card catalog. See MAIN ENTRY, CORPORATE ENTRY, ADDED ENTRY, SUBJECT ENTRY, TITLE ENTRY.

FILING: Arranging cards or other materials in a definite order. The order may be alphabetical, numerical or classified.

FIRST INDENTATION: The distance from the left edge of a catalog card at which, according to a special rule, the author heading begins.

FLYLEAF: The first or last sheet in a bound book, usually blank.

FORM HEADING: A heading used to designate the form of certain classes of material, such as encyclopedias and dictionaries, periodicals, etc.

FORM TITLE: See CONVENTIONAL TITLE.

FORMAT: The physical form of a work: size, binding, printing.

GUIDE CARD: A heavier card with a tab which projects above the other cards in the catalog or index file. Letters, numbers, words or names are written on the top of the guide card to show what cards are directly behind it.

HANGING INDENTATION: The indentation of all lines except the first line to the second indentation. It is used when the title is the main entry.

HEADING: A word, name or phrase at the top of the catalog card used as the primary element of identification.

HISTORY CARD: A catalog card which gives the history of successive names used by a person or organization.

HOLDINGS: The library's collection of books and other materials.

IMPRINT: Publication information about a work: place, date, and publisher; usually found at the bottom of the title page.

INDENTATION: A fixed number of typewriter spaces from the left edge of a catalog card at which typing begins.

INFORMATION FILE: A card file of references to sources of information on various topics.

INTERNATIONAL STANDARD BOOK NUMBER (ISBN): A code number assigned by publishers to a specific title or edition of a title. May be used as identification in ordering books.

INVENTORY: Checking bookshelves with the shelf list or other records of library holdings to determine whether any items are missing.

INVOICE: An itemized list of goods shipped to a buyer, stating quantities, prices, shipping charges, etc.

JOINT AUTHOR; JOINT EDITOR: One or more people who work together with a main author or editor in preparing a work for publication.

LC: The Library of Congress, U.S.A.
LC CARD: See LIBRARY OF CONGRESS CARD.
LEAF; LEAVES: Pages of a publication. Each leaf usually has a page of text on each side.
LIBRARY COLLECTION: See COLLECTION.
LIBRARY OF CONGRESS CARD: Commonly called LC card. A catalog card prepared for Library of Congress use; printed and sold to other libraries.
LIST PRICE: The retail price established by a publisher, listed in catalogs and bibliographies.
LOCATION SYMBOL; LOCATION MARK: A letter, sign or other symbol used on books or other materials in special collections which are shelved out of classification order; for example, the reference collection.
MAIN ENTRY: A full catalog entry, usually the author entry, giving all the information necessary for complete identification of the work. It usually contains the tracing of all other entries made for the work.
MATERIAL or LIBRARY MATERIAL: Inclusive term for books, periodicals, pamphlets, maps, films, etc. - all the items which a library acquires.
MICROFORM: Reproductions in miniature, on transparent or opaque stock, of printed materials. Reduction is usually about 1/20 of the original. Various forms include microfilm, microfiche, microcard and microprint.
MNEMONICS: Symbols in the notation of a classification system which are easily learned because they have the same meaning wherever they occur.
MONOGRAPH: A short work on a single subject or class of subjects, usually detailed in treatment but not extensive in scope.
MONOGRAPHIC SERIES: Separate nonfiction works issued, perhaps at different times, under a collective title; may or may not be a numbered series.
NOTATION: A system of letters, numbers or other symbols used to distinguish one subject from another in a scheme of classification.
NOTE: A phrase or sentence added to the catalog card to explain a feature of the work cataloged.
OPEN ENTRY: A catalog entry for a periodical or set of volumes which is still being published. The latest numbers of volumes and dates are written in pencil so that they can be changed as more volumes are received. Opposite of CLOSED ENTRY.
ORDER FORM: A printed set of forms, usually duplicate or triplicate, for ordering library material.
OUT-OF-PRINT: All copies printed have been sold; the item is no longer available from the publisher.
PAGE: In a book or other publication, one side of a leaf or sheet.
PAMPHLET: A publication of less than 50 (or 100) pages, usually on one specific subject.
PAMPHLET FILE: A file of large drawers in which are arranged folders containing pamphlets, pictures, clippings, maps. Sometimes called VERTICAL FILE.
PAPERBACK: A book bound in paper with a flexible cover instead of a hard cloth cover.
PERIODICAL: A publication with a distinctive title that appears in successive numbers, or parts, and at regular intervals, for example, weekly, monthly,

quarterly, and as a rule for an indefinite time. Sometimes called a journal or magazine. It generally has articles by several contributors.

PERIODICAL INDEX: An index to the contents of a periodical or a group of periodicals.

PHONODISC: A recording of sound on a disc; a round, flat record.

PHONOTAPE: A recording of sound on tape.

PREPARATIONS: The part of library work concerned with the physical preparation of a publication for library use; includes such tasks as marking spine, pasting in pocket, etc.

PROCESS SLIP: A slip of paper or a card used by the cataloger in preparing information to be used in making catalog cards..

PROCESSING: Includes the work of acquiring, cataloging and preparing library materials.

PSEUDONYM: Name taken by an author to conceal his identity.

PUBLICATION DATE: The year when a book is published. It may be the same as the copyright date or the date of a later reprinting.

PUBLISHER: The person, firm, or corporate body responsible for the issue of a book or other printed matter.

PUBLISHER'S CATALOG: A list compiled by a publisher showing his current publications.

RECORDING: See PHONODISC or PHONOTAPE.

REFERENCE BOOK: A book of general information such as an encyclopedia or dictionary, used to obtain specific information quickly. Reference books are restricted to use in the library.

REPRINT: A new printing of a publication which is the same as an earlier one in content; the format may be the same or different. Sometimes means a cheaper edition of an earlier work.

REQUISITION FORM: A form, usually on index cards, used as a consideration file before books are purchased, which contains all necessary order information.

REVISE: To check or review work done, such as checking typing or filing, or to correct errors.

REVISED EDITION; REVISION: A publication containing new or changed material.

SECOND INDENTATION: The distance from the left edge of a catalog card at which, according to a special rule, the title begins.

"SEE ALSO" REFERENCE: A catalog or index card referring from a term or name to a related term or name where more material will be found.

"SEE" REFERENCE: A catalog or index card referring from a term or name under which no entries are listed to a term or name under which entries for that subject or name will be found.

SEQUEL: A work, complete in itself, that continues a narrative from an earlier work.

SERIAL: A publication issued in successive parts at regular or irregular intervals and intended to continue indefinitely. The parts may or may not be numbered. Includes periodicals, newspapers, reports, bulletins, etc.

SERIES: Separate works that are published at different times but belong under a collective series title, often with numbered volumes.

SERIES NOTE: A note on the catalog card, usually in parentheses after the collation, noting the series of which the work is a part.
SERIES TITLE: The collective title of the series to which a work belongs.
SET: A work of two or more volumes.
SHELF LIST: A catalog of the books in the library arranged by call number in the order of the books on the shelves, with a card for each title.
SHELF READING: Checking books on the shelves to be sure they are arranged in correct order.
SPINE: The flexible "back" of the book which holds the two cover boards together and protects the binding. Most books have the title and author's name on the spine so as to be easily identified when shelved.
STACKS: Standing shelves for books; the shelved collection; area in which materials are stored.
STAFF: In a library, all the people who work under the direction of the librarian.
SUBJECT: The topic or field of knowledge discussed in a book; the name, word, or phrase used as a catalog entry which indicates the subject content of the work cataloged.
SUBJECT ANALYTIC: A heading or catalog entry identifying the subject of a part of a work.
SUBJECT CATALOG: A file of subject cards arranged by subject entries.
SUBJECT CATALOGING: Assigning a term or terms to each book which shows the topic or field of knowledge discussed in a book.
SUBJECT ENTRY: A card with the name of the subject on the top line, above the author line, and at the second indentation.
SUBJECT HEADING: A word or a group of words indicating a subject under which all material dealing with the same theme is entered in a catalog.
SUBTITLE: The explanatory part of a title following the main title.
THIRD INDENTATION: The distance from the left edge of a catalog card at which, according to special rules, certain parts of the description begin or continue.
TITLE: The name given to a book on the title page.
TITLE ANALYTIC: A catalog entry under the title identifying the title of a part of a book or other work.
TITLE AND AUTHOR ANALYTIC: The catalog entry at the top of the card which gives the title and author of a part of a publication.
TITLE ENTRY: The record of a work in a catalog or a bibliography entered under the title. It may be a main entry under title for a work that does not have a distinct author or editor; for example, a periodical entry is usually under the title, or it may be an added entry.
TITLE PAGE: The page at the beginning of a book which gives author, title, publisher's name and publication date. Often there is an earlier page, called the half-title, which gives the title or name of the series to which the book belongs.
TRACING: A list on the main entry card of all other catalog cards which have been made for a book, such as title, editor, subjects, etc.
UNIFORM TITLE: See CONVENTIONAL TITLE.

UNIT CARD: One of a set of catalog cards, all of which are alike until the added entries are added at the top of the card.

VERTICAL FILE: See PAMPHLET FILE.

VISIBLE FILE: A series of frames in which cards may be mounted with the headings visible one above another; used as a checking file for periodicals.

WANT LIST: A list of books or other materials that would be desirable for the library when funds are available.

WEED: To remove worn, outdated or useless materials from a library collection.

WITHDRAWAL: The process of removing from library records all entries for a book no longer in the library.

WORK MARK or WOR4 NUMBER: The first letter of the title of a work, excluding articles, placed after the Cutter number or below the author letters.

WORK SLIP: A slip of paper or card on which the cataloger writes directions and information necessary to prepare catalog entries, cross references, etc.

YEARBOOK: A work issued annually; for example, an almanac.

II. REFERENCE BOOKS

Every library should have books which contain information such as is found in encyclopedias, dictionaries, atlases, handbooks and others. Reference books are revised and brought up-to-date frequently, many annually. In this bibliography, when dates of publication are not given, the most recent edition is desired. Only books currently in print are listed.

Since libraries are often the recipients of gift books, several bibliographies to assist in the process of selection and weeding are included. It is not necessary to purchase all of them, but they may be found in larger libraries.

In all subject areas, many titles are available, but in this list only those with larger coverage, those which are less expensive and those which are easily obtainable have been included.

BIBLIOGRAPHIES

Books in Print. New York, Bowker, annual-
   Lists books available from American publishers in author, title, and subject volumes. Also available, *British Books in Print.* London, Whitaker, annual- and *Paperbound Books in Print.* New York, Bowker, current-

Children's Catalog. New York, Wilson, latest-
   A classified catalog of books useful on the elementary school level.

Cumulative Book Index. New York, Wilson, cumulative-
   A world-wide list of books in the English language.

Katz, Bill and Berry Gargal. *Magazines for Libraries.* 2nd ed. New York, Bowker, 1972. Supplement, 1974.
   Provides lists of periodicals in various subject areas with bibliographical information and evaluation useful for selection. An extensive list with addresses but no evaluations is *Ulrich's International Periodicals Directory.* 16th ed. New York, Bowker, 1975.

Sheehy, Eugene P. *Guide to Reference Books.* 9th ed. Chicago, American Library Association, 1976.
   One of the most comprehensive lists of reference works with brief annotations for each. Coverage is international and includes books in many languages.

Standard Catalog for High School Libraries. New York, Wilson, latest-
   A good selection guide for high school level books. Also available is *Junior High School Library Catalog.* New York, Wilson, latest-

Wynar, Bohdan. *Reference Books in Paperback.* 2nd ed. Littleton, Libraries Unlimited, 1976.
   Important reference books available in cheaper editions.

ENCYCLOPEDIAS

Encyclopedias are published in almost every language. If English is not the language of your area, you should consider encyclopedias written in your local language. One or two sets are adequate at first.

Encyclopedia Americana. New York, Americana Corporation, latest-
   Has short articles except for major subjects, with emphasis on modern scientific and technological developments.

Encyclopaedia Britannica. Chicago, Encyclopaedia Britannica, latest-
   Scholarly articles with good bibliographies.

Collier's Encyclopedia. New York, Collier, latest-
   Emphasizes modern subjects. Well illustrated.

Compton's Pictured Encyclopedia. Chicago, Compton, latest-
   A good juvenile encyclopedia with graded subjects.

World Book Encyclopedia. Chicago, Field Enterprises, latest-
   An outstanding juvenile encyclopedia, but useful for all ages.

DICTIONARIES

Many language dictionaries are available; the following are suggested.

Cassell's French Dictionary. New York, Funk and Wagnalls, 1973.

Cassell's Italian Dictionary. New York, Funk and Wagnalls, 1967.

Cassell's New German Dictionary. New York, Funk and Wagnalls, 1971.

Cassell's Spanish Dictionary. New York, Funk and Wagnalls, 1968.

Fowler, Henry Watson. *Concise Oxford Dictionary of Current English.* 6th ed.
   London, Oxford University Press, 1976.
   Emphasis is on British usage for countries where this is preferred.

Webster's New Collegiate Dictionary. Rev. ed. Springfield, Merriam Co., 1976.
   A good desk dictionary which is revised frequently to include new words introduced into the language. Others recommended are: *New College Dictionary.* New York, Random House, 1966 and *Funk and Wagnalls Standard College Dictionary.* New York, Funk and Wagnalls, 1974.

Webster's Third New International Dictionary of the English Language. Springfield, Merriam Co., 1971.
   Unabridged dictionary containing 450,000 words emphasizing modern usage.

If English is the language of your country, this is recommended.

ATLASES AND GAZETTEERS

Road maps, local maps of your area and country are useful supplements to a collection of atlases.

Goode's World Atlas. 14th ed. Chicago, Rand McNally, 1974.
   Physical, political and economic maps of the world. Other atlases are published by Rand McNally and The Hammond Co.

Shepherd, William R. *Shepherd's Historical Atlas.* 9th ed. New York, Harper & Row, 1973.
   Maps covering world history since 1450.

Webster's New Geographical Dictionary. Rev. ed. Springfield, Merriam Co., 1972.
   A gazetteer which identifies geographical places and gives pronunciation.

Wright, George Ernest and Filson, Floyd. *Westminster Historical Atlas to The Bible.* Rev. ed. Philadelphia, Westminster, 1956.
   There are many others on this subject including Aharoni, Yohanan and Avi-Yonah, Michael. *Macmillan Atlas.* New York, Macmillan, 1968.

HANDBOOKS AND ALMANACS

Stateman's Yearbook. New York, St. Martin's Press, annual- and London, Macmillan.
   A useful tool which covers governments, areas, population, education, religion, industry and social welfare for all countries of the world.

World Almanac and Book of Facts. New York, Doubleday, annual-
   A wealth of factual information of all kinds; coverage is world-wide. Similar information is found in *Information Please Almanac.* New York, Simon & Schuster, annual- and *Whitaker's Almanack.* London, Whitaker, annual-

U.S. Bureau of The Census. *Statistical Abstract of the U.S.* Washington, Government Printing Office, annual-
   A digest of statistical information compiled by the statistical agencies of the U.S. government as well as private agencies. Every country may have a similar handbook which may be obtained from the local government.

U.S. Government Organization Manual. Washington, Government Printing Office, current-
  Each country may have similar publication.

U.S. Congress. *Official Congressional Directory.* Washington, Government Printing Office, current-
  Biographies and addresses of U.S. congressmen, foreign diplomats and consular officials. Comparable directories in other countries.

BIOGRAPHICAL WORKS

Books about people range from those attempting to cover all the world in every era to specialized works relating to particular localities or professions. It is necessary for each library to decide what its particular needs are. *Who's Who* volumes are published in many countries and for various occupations.

Current Biography. New York, Wilson, annual-
  Contains sketches of people prominent in the news, national and international.
  It appears monthly, but the bound annual volumes are more useful.

Webster's Biographical Dictionary. Springfield, Merriam Co., 1964.
  Brief biographical lists of prominent people, living and dead, of all nations and all times. A useful work.

ART REFERENCE WORKS

Encyclopedia of World Art. New York, McGraw-Hill, 1959.
  A monumental work covering architecture, painting, sculpture and other arts world-wide. Half of each of the fifteen volumes consists of illustrative plates.

Gardner, Helen. *Art Through The Ages.* 6th ed. New York, Harcourt, 1975.
  A history of art through the ages.

MUSIC REFERENCE WORKS

Apel, Willi. *Harvard Dictionary of Music.* 2nd ed. Cambridge, Harvard University Press, 1969
  Comprehensive list of musical terms and definitions.

Thompson, Oscar. *International Cyclopedia of Music and Musicians.* 10th rev. ed. New York, Dodd, Mead, 1975
  A useful one volume encyclopedia of music and musicians. A more

comprehensive work is *Grove's Dictionary of Music and Musicians.* New York, St. Martin's Press, 1954. 10 volumes. This can sometimes be found in second-hand book stores.

SCIENCE REFERENCE WORKS

This is a very broad field and recent books are necessary to keep up with modern developments. Many paperback editions are available for rocks, trees, flowers, birds, stars, etc.

Dorlans's Illustrated Medical Dictionary. 25th ed. Philadelphia, Saunders, 1974.
Dictionary of terms in the medical sciences.

Van Nostrand's Scientific Encyclopedia. 5th ed. New York, Van Nostrand Reinhold, 1976.
A comprehensive work which covers basic and applied sciences.

LITERATURE REFERENCE BOOKS

Bartlett, John. *Familiar Quotations.* Secaucus, Citadel, latest-
Chronologically arranged quotations with a word index. Others recommended are: Stevenson, Burton. *Home Book of Quotations.* Rev. ed. New York, Dodd, 1967 and *Oxford Dictionary of Quotations.* London, Oxford University Press, 1953.

Benet, William R. *The Reader's Encyclopedia.* 2nd ed. New York, Crowell, 1965
An encyclopedia of world literature covering trends, movements, characters in fiction, plots and biography.

Granger's Index to Poetry. New York, Columbia University Press, latest-
Lists titles, first lines, authors and subjects found in poetry anthologies.

Roget's International Thesaurus. New York, Crowell, latest-
Groups words according to ideas which they express; helpful to writers.

RELIGIOUS REFERENCE WORKS

Alexander, David and Patricia. *Eerdmans' Handbook to The Bible.* Grand Rapids, Eerdmans, 1973.
A well illustrated handbook to the Bible. Other useful ones are: Tenney, Merrill C. *Zondervan Pictorial Bible Dictionary.* Grand Rapids, Zondervan, 1969 and Unger, Merrill F. *Unger's Bible Handbook.* Chicago, Moody Press, 1966

Barber, Cyril. *The Minister's Library.* Grand Rapids, Baker, 1973
   A good annotated bibliography of books in the religious field.

Cruden, Alexander. *Cruden's Unabridged Concordance.* Grand Rapids, Baker, 1953
   A complete concordance to the Bible including proper names and a concordance to the apocryphal books. The scholar will probably prefer Strong, James. *Exhaustive Concordance of The Bible.* Nashville, Abingdon, 1958 or Young, Robert. *Young's Analytical Concordance to The Bible.* Rev. ed. Grand Rapids, Eerdmans, 1955.
   Concordances are available to *The Living Bible* and the Revised Version.

Henry, Matthew. *Commentary on The Whole Bible.* Old Tappan, Revell, n.d.
   One of many excellent Bible commentaries. Others are listed in the bibliographies of Barber, Merchant and Smith.

Merchant, Harish. *Encounter with Books; A Guide to Christian Reading.* Downers Grove, Inter-Varsity, 1970.
   A good bibliography for selection of Christian books.

Orr, James. *International Standard Bible Encyclopedia.* Rev. ed. Grand Rapids, Eerdmans, 1930.
   An older work, but useful for its conservative scholarship.

Smith, Wilbur M. *Profitable Bible Study.* Grand Rapids, Baker, 1971.
   A helpful bibliography by a great Christian scholar.

Tenney, Merrill C. *New Zondervan Pictorial Encyclopedia of The Bible.* Grand Rapids, Zondervan, 1974. Five volumes.

REFERENCE WORKS IN HISTORY

This represents a broad area. It is important to concentrate on histories of your area, country and continent.

Langer, William L. *Encyclopedia of World History.* 5th ed. Boston, Houghton Mifflin, 1972.
   A chronological handbook of world history, ancient, medieval and modern.

PERIODICAL INDEXES

Magazines are an important source of information, but in order to locate a specific article on a given subject, it is necessary to use cumulative indexes which cover many titles for a period of time. Many indexing services are available which cover a particular subject or discipline. In order to make an index useful, it is necessary that the library subscribe to a large number of periodicals included in the index. Two are suggested.

Abridged Readers' Guide to Periodical Literature. New York, Wilson, 1936-
   Approximately 40 periodicals of general interest for a small library are included. The publication appears monthly, with periodic cumulations.

Christian Periodical Index. Buffalo, Christian Librarians' Fellowship, 1956-
   Indexes approximately 40 periodicals by author and by subject, with a book review section for current books. These periodicals are chosen for their value to people involved in Christian ministries or in the field of evangelical Christian literature. The index appears quarterly with cumulations.

III. BIBLIOGRAPHY

GENERAL

Aldrich, Ella Virginia. *Using Theological Books and Libraries,* by E.V. Aldrich and T.E. Camp. Englewood Cliffs, Prentice-Hall, 1963.
Bernard, Genore H. *How To Organize and Operate A Small Library.* Fort Atkinson, Highsmith, 1975.
Newhall, Jannette E. *A Theological Library Manual.* London, The Theological Education Fund, 1970.
Towns, Elmer L. *Successful Church Libraries,* by Elmer L. Towns and Cyril J. Barber. Grand Rapids, Baker, 1971.

BOOK SELECTION

Barber, Cyril J. *The Minister's Library.* Grand Rapids, Baker, 1974.
Barton, Mary N. *Reference Books; A Brief Guide.* 7th ed. Baltimore, MD, Enoch Pratt Library, 1970.
Evangelical Teacher Training Association. *Books for Christian Educators.* Wheaton, Evangelical Teacher Training Association.
Merchant, Harish. *Encounter With Books; A Guide to Christian Reading.* Downers Grove, Inter-Varsity, 1970.
Morris, Raymond P. *A Theological Book List.* New ed. London, Greeno Hadden, 1971.

CATALOGING

Akers, Susan Grey. *Akers' Simple Library Cataloging,* by Susan G. Akers and Arthur Curley. 6th completely rev. ed. Metuchen, Scarecrow Press, 1976.
Anglo-American Cataloging Rules. North American Text. Ed. by C. Sumner Spalding. Chicago, American Library Association, 1967.
Haykin, David J. *Subject Headings: A Practical Guide.* Ash Lee, ed. Reprint of 1951 ed. Boston, Gregg.
Immroth, John Philip. *Library Cataloging; A Guide for A Basic Course,* by John P. Immroth and Jay E. Daily. Metuchen, Scarecrow, 1971.
Piercy, Esther J. *Commonsense Cataloging; A Manual for The Organization of Books and Other Materials in School and Small Public Libraries.* 2nd ed. Revised by Marian Sanner. New York, Wilson, 1974
Sears, Minnie Earl. *Sears List of Subject Headings.* 11th ed. by Barbara Westby. New York, Wilson, 1977.
Wynar, Bohdan S. *Introduction to Cataloging and Classification.* 5th ed. Littleton, Libraries Unlimited, 1976.

CLASSIFICATION

Cutter, Charles A. *Cutter-Sanborn Three-Figure Author Table.* Swanson-Swift Revision. Chicopee, H.R. Huntting, 1969.

Dewey, Melvil. *Dewey Decimal Classification and Relative Index.* Ed. 18. Albany, Forest Press, 1971.
Dewey, Melvil. *Abridged Dewey Decimal Classification and Relative Index.* Ed. 10. Albany, Forest Press, 1971.
Dewey, Melvil. *200 (Religion) Class.* Reprinted from Edition 18 Unabridged. Nashville, Broadman, 1971.

Note: Translations in many languages are available of all or part of *Dewey Decimal Classification.* Obtain information about them from your national Library Association or from Forest Press. The following are examples:
Classification Decimale de Dewey et Index. Version francaise integrale. Albany, Forest Press, 1974
A Hindi selective abridgement is available from The Universal Book Stall, 5 Ansari Road, New Delhi-110 002 India.
A new Spanish translation will be published in 1979, available from Forest Press.

TECHNICAL PROCESSING

Bloomberg, Marty. *Introduction to Technical Services for Library Technicians,* by Marty Bloomberg and G. Edward Evans. 2nd ed. Littleton, Libraries Unlimited, 1974
Daily, Jay E. *Cataloging Workbook for Library Technical Assistants.* Ed. by Mildred S. Myers. Washington, Gryphon, 1972

FILING

American Library Association. *ALA Rules for Filing Catalog Cards.* Pauline A. Seely, Editor. 2nd ed., abr. Chicago, American Library Association, 1968.
Library of Congress. Processing Department. *Filing Rules for the Dictionary Catalogs of The Library of Congress.* Washington, Card Division, Library of Congress, 1956.

NONBOOK MATERIALS

GENERAL

Association for Educational Communications and Technology. *Standards for Cataloging Nonprint Materials.* 3rd ed. Washington, National Education Assocation Publication Sales Section, 1972.

Brown, James W. *Audio-Visual Instruction: Technology, Media and Methods,* by James W. Brown, Richard B. Lewis and others. 5th ed. New York, McGraw-Hill, 1977.
Hicks, Warren B. *Developing Multi-Media Libraries,* by Warren B. Hicks and Alma M. Tillin. New York, Bowker, 1970.
Kujoth, Jean Spealman, ed. *Readings in Nonbook Librarianship.* Metuchen, Scarecrow Press, 1968.
Rufsvold, Margaret I. *Guides to Educational Media,* by Margaret I. Rufsvold and Carolyn Guss. 3rd ed. Chicago, American Library Association, 1971.
Weihs, Jean Riddle. *Nonbook Materials: The Organization of Integrated Collections.* 1st ed. by Jean Riddle Weihs, Shirley Lewis, Janet Macdonald. Ottawa, Canadian Library Association, 1973.

PAMPHLETS

Gould, Geraldine N. *How to Organize and Maintain The Library Picture/Pamphlet File,* by Geraldine N. Gould and Ithmer C. Wolfe. Dobbs Ferry, Oceana, 1968.
Ireland, Norma Olin. *The Pamphlet File in School, College and Public Libraries.* Westwood, Faxon, 1954.
Miller, Shirley. *The Vertical File and Its Satellites; A Handbook of Acquisition, Processing and Organization.* Littleton, Libraries Unlimited, 1971.

PAMPHLET JOBBERS

Bacon Pamphlet Service, Inc. East Chatham, NY 12060
Vertical File Materials, Box 481, Lincoln, NE 68501
William-Frederick Press, 55 E. 86th St. New York, NY 10028

PAMPHLET SOURCES

Kenworth, Leonard S. *Free and Inexpensive Materials on World Affairs.* New York, Teachers College, 1969.
Monahan, Robert. *Free and Inexpensive Materials.* Belmont, Fearon, 1973.
Vertical File Index. Monthly except August. Bronx, Wilson.

SERIALS

Serials in Microform. Xerox University Microfilms, 300 North Zeeb Road, Ann Arbor, MI 48106

MICROFORMS

Introduction to Micrographics. National Microfilm Association, Suite 1101, 8728 Colesville, Road, Silver Springs, MD 20910

EQUIPMENT

Audio-Visual Equipment Directory. National Audio-Visual Association, Fairfax, VA 05454

Buyer's Guide to Microfilm Equipment. National Microfilm Association, Suite 1101, 8728 Colesville Road, Silver Springs, MD 20910

PICTURES

Dane, William Jerald, *The Picture Collection: Subject Headings.* 6th ed. Hamden, Shoe String Press, 1968.

Ireland, Norma Olin. *The Picture File in School, College and Public Libaries.* Rev. and enl. ed. Westwood, Faxon, 1952.

RECORDINGS

Code for Cataloging Music and Phono-Records. Prepared by a Joint Committee of the Music Library Association and the A.L.A. Division of Cataloging and Classification. Chicago, American Library Association, 1958.

Pearson, Mary D. *Recordings in The Public Library.* Chicago, American Library Association, 1963.

Schwann Record and Tape Guide. W. Schwann, Inc. 137 Newbury St., Boston, MA 02116

PRESERVATION OF MATERIALS

Lydenberg, Harry M. *The Care and Repair of Books,* by Harry M. Lydenberg and John Archer. Rev. by John Alden. New York, Bowker, 1960.

LIBRARY BUILDINGS

Metcalf, Keyes D. *Planning Academic and Research Library Buildings.* New York, McGraw-Hill, 1965.

> A comprehensive manual covering all aspects of library building planning, designed as an aid to those without experience in such a task. While it deals with designs for larger buildings, it is a valuable resource for any size project, giving basic data on procedure and accepted standards for space requirements.

Newhall, Jannette, "The Library Building," pp. 134-143 in her *A Theological Library Manual.* London, The Theological Education Fund, 1970.

> Includes basic measurements for book shelves, tables, chairs, aisles, and practical suggestions for planning office, work and storage areas, a section on lighting and a section on improving older buildings.

Schultz, Susan A. "Some notes on The Preparation of A Library Building Program," pp. 3, 4 in *The Christian Librarian,* April, 1974.

> A copy may be obtained from The Christian Librarians' Fellowship.

IV. PUBLISHERS

ABINGDON PRESS, 201 Eighth Ave. S., Nashville, TN 37202
ALLENSON, ALEC R., INC., 635 E. Ogden Ave., Box 31, Naperville, IL 60540
AMERICAN BOOK CO., 135 W. 50th St., New York, NY 10020
AMERICAN LIBRARY ASSOCIATION, 50 E. Huron St., Chicago, IL 60611
AMERICANA CORP., 575 Lexington Ave., New York, NY 10022
APPLETON-CENTURY-CROFTS, 292 Madison Ave., New York, NY 10017
ASSOCIATION PRESS, 291 Broadway, New York, NY 10007
BAKER BOOK HOUSE, 1019 Wealthy St. S.E., Grand Rapids, MI 49506
BANNER OF TRUTH TRUST, 3 Murrayfield Road, Edinburgh EH12 6EL, Scotland
BEACON HILL PRESS, 2923 Troost Ave., P.O. Box 527, Kansas City, MO 64141
BETHANY FELLOWSHIP, INC., 6820 Auto Club Rd., Minneapolis, MN 55438
BETHANY PRESS, 2640 Pine Blvd., Box 179, St. Louis, MO 63166
BIBLO AND TANNEN BOOKSELLERS & PUBLISHERS, 63 Fourth Ave., New York, NY 10003
*BLACKWELL, B.H., LTD., 5 Alfred St., Oxford, England
BOWKER, R.R., 1180 Avenue of the Americas, New York, NY 10036
*BRILL, E.J., Oude Rijn 33A, Leiden, Netherlands
    or   41 Museum St., London, WC1A 1LX, England
BROADMAN PRESS, 127 Ninth Ave. N., Nashville, TN 37203
BROWN, WILLIAM C., CO., 2460 Kerper Blvd., Dubuque, IA 52001
CAREY, WILLIAM, LIBRARY, 1705 N. Sierra Bonita Ave., Pasadena, CA 91104
CHRISTIAN LIBRARIANS' FELLOWSHIP, Houghton College, 910 Union Rd., Buffalo, NY 11224
CHRISTIAN LITERATURE CRUSADE, Ft. Washington, PA 19034
CHRISTIAN PUBLICATIONS, INC., 25 S. Tenth St., Harrisburg, PA 17101
CITADEL PRESS, 120 Enterprise Ave., Secaucus, NJ 07094
CLARK, T. AND T., 38 George St., Edinburgh, EH2, Scotland
COLLIER, P.F., INC., 866 Third Ave., New York, NY 10022
COLUMBIA UNIVERSITY PRESS, 562 W. 113th St., New York, NY 10025
COMPTON, F.E., CO., 425 N. Michigan Ave., Chicago, IL 60611
CONCORDIA PUBLISHING HOUSE, 3558 S. Jefferson Ave., St. Louis, MO 63118
COOK, DAVID C., PUBLISHING CO., 850 N. Grove Ave., Elgin, IL 60120
COVENANT PRESS, 5101 N. Francisco Ave., Chicago, IL 60625
CROWELL, THOMAS Y., CO., 666 Fifth Ave., New York, NY 10019
DENISON, T.S., & CO., 9601 Newton Ave., S., Minneapolis, MN 55431
DODD, MEAD & CO., 79 Madison Ave., New York, NY 10016
DOUBLEDAY & CO., INC., 501 Franklin Ave., Garden City, NY 11530
EERDMANS, WM. B., PUBLISHING CO., 255 Jefferson Ave., S.E., Grand Rapids, MI 49502
ENCYCLOPAEDIA BRITANNICA, INC., 425 N. Michigan Ave., Chicago, IL 60611

EVANGELICAL TEACHER TRAINING ASSN., P.O. Box 327, Wheaton, IL 60187
*FAXON, F.W., CO., INC., 15 Southwest Park, Westwood, MA 02090
FEARON PUBLISHERS, INC., 6 Davis Dr., Belmont CA 94002
FIELD ENTERPRISES EDUCATIONAL CORP., 510 Merchandise Mart Plaza, Chicago, IL 60654
FOREST PRESS, INC., 85 Watervliet Ave., Albany, NY 12206
FORTRESS PRESS, 2900 Queen Lane, Philadelphia, PA 19129
FREE CHURCH PUBLICATIONS, 1515 E. 66th St., Minneapolis, MN 55423
FRIENDSHIP PRESS, 475 Riverside Dr., New York, NY 10027
FUNK & WAGNALLS CO., 666 Fifth Ave., New York, NY 10019
GOSPEL LIGHT PUBLICATIONS, 110 W. Broadway, Glendale, CA 91204
GOSPEL PUBLISHING HOUSE, 1445 Boonville Ave., Springfield, MO 65802
GREENO, HADDEN & CO., LTD., 61 Roseland St., Somerville, MA 02143
GREGG PRESS, INC., 70 Lincoln St., Boston, MA 02111
GRYPHON HOUSE, P.O. Box 217, Mt. Ranier, MD 20822
HAMMOND, INC., 515 Valley St., Maplewood, NJ 07040
HARCOURT BRACE JOVANOVICH, INC., 757 Third Ave., New York, NY 10017
HARPER & ROW PUBLISHERS, INC., 10 E. 53rd St., New York, NY 10022
HARVARD UNIVERSITY PRESS, 79 Garden St., Cambridge, MA 02138
HERALD PRESS, 616 Walnut Ave., Scottdale, PA 15683
HIGHSMITH CO., INC., P.O. Box 25, Fort Atkinson, WI 53538
HOLT, RINEHART AND WINSTON, INC., 383 Madison Ave., New York, NY 10017
HOUGHTON MIFFLIN CO., 2 Park St., Boston, MA 02107
HUNTTING, H.R., CO., 300 Burnett Road, Chicopee, MA 01020
INTER-VARSITY PRESS, P.O. Box F, Downers Grove, IL 60515
JOHN KNOX PRESS, 341 Ponce de Leon Ave., N.E., Atlanta, GA 30308
JOSSEY-BASS, INC., 433 California St., San Francisco, CA 94104
JUDSON PRESS, Valley Forge, PA 19481
KREGEL PUBLICATIONS, P.O. Box 2607, Grand Rapids, MI 49501
LIBRARIES UNLIMITED, INC., P.O. Box 263, Littleton, CO 80120
LIGHT AND LIFE PRESS, Winona Lake, IN 46590
LOIZEAUX BROS., INC., 1238 Corlies Ave., P.O. Box 70, Neptune, NJ 07753
McGRAW-HILL BOOK CO., 1221 Avenue of the Americas, New York, NY 10036
MACMILLAN PUBLISHING CO., INC., 866 Third Ave., New York, NY 10022
MERRIAM, G & C., CO., 47 Federal St., Springfield, MA 01101
MOODY PRESS, 820 N. LaSalle St., Chicago, IL 60610
NATIONAL GEOGRAPHIC SOCIETY, 17th & M Sts. N.W., Washington, DC 20036
NELSON, THOMAS, INC., P.O. Box 946, 407 Seventh Ave., S., Nashville, TN 37203
OCEANA PUBLICATIONS, INC., 75 Main St., Dobbs Ferry, NY 10522
OXFORD UNIVERSITY PRESS, INC., 1600 Pollitt Dr., Fairlawn, NJ 07410
        or   Ely House, 370 Dover St., London, WlX4H, England
PRENTICE-HALL INTERNATIONAL, INC., 301 Sylvan Ave., Englewood Cliffs, NJ 07632

PRESBYTERIAN & REFORMED PUBLISHING CO., Box 817, Phillipsburg, NJ 08865
PRINCETON UNIVERSITY PRESS, 41 William St., Princeton, NJ 08540
RAND McNALLY & CO., P.O. Box 7600, Chicago, IL 60680
RANDOM HOUSE, INC., 201 E. 50th St., New York, NY 10022
REVELL, FLEMING H., CO., 184 Central Ave., Old Tappan, NJ 07675
ST. MARTIN'S PRESS, INC., 175 Fifth Ave., New York, NY 10010
SAUNDERS, W.B., CO., W. Washington Square, Philadelphia, PA 19105
SCARECROW PRESS, INC., 52 Liberty St., Box 656, Metuchen, NJ 08840
SCOTT, FORESMAN & CO., 1900 E. Lake Ave., Glenview, IL 60025
SCRIBNER'S, CHARLES, SONS, 597 Fifth Ave., New York, NY 10017
SCRIPTURE PRESS, 1825 College Ave., Wheaton, IL 60187
SEABURY PRESS, INC., 815 Second Ave., New York, NY 10017
SHOE STRING PRESS, INC., 995 Sherman Ave., Hamden, CT 06514
SIMON & SCHUSTER, INC., 1230 Ave. of the Americas, New York, NY 10020
SPCK BOOKSHOP, 69 Great Peter St., London, SW1, England
STANDARD PUBLISHING, 8121 Hamilton Ave., Cincinnati, OH 45231
TEACHERS COLLEGE PRESS, Columbia University, 1234 Amsterdam Ave., New York, NY 10027
THE THEOLOGICAL EDUCATION FUND, 13 London Road, Bromley, Kent, England
THIN, JAMES, 53-59 South Bridge, Edinburgh, Scotland
TYNDALE HOUSE PUBLISHERS, 336 Gundersen Dr., Wheaton, IL 60187
UNITED CHURCH PRESS, 287 Park Ave. S., New York, NY 10010
U.S. GOVERNMENT PRINTING OFFICE, Div. of Public Documents, Washington, DC 20402
VAN NOSTRAND REINHOLD CO., 135 W. 50th St., New York, NY 10020
WARNER PRESS, 1200 E. Fifth St., Anderson, IN 46011
WESTERN PUBLISHING CO., 850 Third Ave., New York, NY 10022
WESTMINSTER PRESS, Room 905, Witherspoon Bldg., Philadelphia, PA 19107
WHITAKER, J. & SONS, LTD., Bedford Square, London, WClB 3JE, England
WILSON, THE H.W., CO., 950 University Ave., Bronx, NY 10052
WORD, INC., P.O. Box 1790, Waco, TX 76703
ZONDERVAN PUBLISHING HOUSE, 1415 Lake Dr. S.E., Grand Rapids, MI 49506

*Handle periodical subscription also.

V. LIBRARY SUPPLIERS

BRO-DART INDUSTRIES, 1609 Memorial Ave., Williamsport, PA 17701
DEMCO LIBRARY SUPPLIES, Box 7488, Madison, WI 53707
GAYLORD BROTHERS, INC., 155 Gifford St., P.O. Box 61, Syracuse, NY 13201
THE HIGHSMITH CO., INC., P.O. Box 25, Fort Atkinson, WI 53538
JOSTEN'S LIBRARY SERVICES DIVISION, 1301 Cliff Road, Burnsville, MN 55337
KEENER RUBBER CO., 721 Alliance Court, Alliance, OH 44601
LIBRARY OF CONGRESS, CARD DIVISION, Bldg. 159, Navy Yard Annex, Washington, DC 20541

VI. BOOK SELECTION POLICY

Alpha Bible College Library

The objectives of Alpha Bible College as stated in the catalog constitute the basis for the book selection policy of the library. The primary aim, "To educate young people for professional (full-time) Christian service (i.e., the ministry, mission field, sacred music and Christian education)" is paramount, supplemented by the philosophy that "every force vital for the development of true Christian character and adequate academic acumen will be brought to focus on the student."

In order to assist in the program for the accomplishment of these goals, the following guidelines for book selection have been adopted:

1. An adequate, up-to-date reference collection is to be maintained.
   A. Standard books of general reference
   B. Reference books useful in specific fields covered by the curriculum

2. Books to support the curriculum, providing duplicates, if necessary for adequate service.
   A. Books concerned with specific areas of a field in which courses are offered
   B. Books concerned with supportive areas of a specific field in which courses are offered
   C. As many of the useful evangelical books in the field of religion as the budget allows
   D. One copy of each current textbook to be kept on Reserve shelf

3. Books to fill in gaps in the collection. This would include not only books to support the viewpoints of the school, but material which would best reflect a wide range of viewpoints in order that students may critically examine varying opinions and aspects of a given subject.

4. Books for a wide range of general education, particularly classics in various fields not specifically related to the curriculum.

5. Recreational reading, which would include not only fiction, but also books on hobbies, sports, travel, biography. Fiction considered for addition to the library collection will be appraised for its classical value, its social significance, or its contribution to a wide range of knowledge of literature.

6. Books related specifically to faculty research will be obtained through interlibrary loan, if possible, unless such books would make a notable contribution to the library collection.

7. No rare books are to be purchased at present in consideration of our limited budget. Gifts will be accepted unless there is a prohibitive restriction accompanying them.

8. Books will be accepted as gifts to the library with the stipulation that there is to be no restriction on their use. If the books are not acceptable or useful for the library collection, they may be sold or discarded. A letter of acknowledgment will be sent to the donor, but no monetary value will be assigned to the gift. It is the donor's responsibility to assign a value to his gift.

9. The selection of books and other materials for the library is a privilege and the responsibility of the entire academic community: administration, faculty, faculty-library committee, librarian, library staff, general staff and students, since all are involved in the process of educating the whole man and no one individual can be expected to be thoroughly acquainted with all the areas of knowledge covered by an academic library. Since it is impossible for the professional librarians to read and personally evaluate every book added to the library, recognized selection aids consulted include the *Catalogue of the Lamont Library at Harvard College,* the ALA *Books for College Libraries* by Voigt and Treyz, *The Reader's Adviser, Choice Opening Day Collection,* and monthly issues of *Choice.* Many periodicals in the religious field serve as reviewing media for religious books, such as *Christianity Today, Eternity, Moody Monthly,* and *Bibliotheca Sacra.*

10. The selection of tape cassettes for the library will follow the guidelines specified for book selection. In addition, when possible, tapes of school-related functions such as missionary conferences and lectureships will be made and placed in the library.

INDEX

Accession number system, 23-24, 111
Accession records, 23-24, 111
Accessioning, 24, 25, 95, 97, 99, 111
Acquisitions
 definition, 111
 jobber, 20, 22
 order routine, 20-21
 organization, 19
 policies and procedures, 20-25
 request form, 19, 20-21
Added entry. See Catalog cards
Administration, 3-8
 budgeting, 6-7
 building, 8
 management, 3-5
 personnel, 5-6
 public relations, 8
 record keeping, 6
Administrative organization, 4
Analytic cards. See Subject analytic cards
Architecture and building
 furnishings, 8, 108-109
 interior design, 8, 108-109
 library program, 107-108
 objectives in, 107
 planning, 107-110
 site, 8, 107
Audio materials. See Recordings
Audio-visual materials. See Nonbook materials; specific types: Motion picture films, Recordings, Slides, etc.
Author entry. See Catalog cards; Filing of catalog cards
Author number. See Cutter number

Bible
 cataloging of, 37-38
 filing of catalog cards, 71-75
 alphabetic arrangement, 71-73
 canonical arrangement, 73-75
Binding, 85
Biographies, classification of, 45
Book buying. See Acquisitions
Book card. See Circulation card
Book jackets
 covering of, 59
 use, 59-60
Book numbers, 44, 112
Book order form. See Acquisitions
Book ordering. See Acquisitions
Book pockets
 format, 57, 58
 location of, 59
Book preparation. See Book jackets, Book pockets, Books, Call numbers, Catalog cards, Circulation cards

Book selection
 factors affecting, 15, 17
 faculty member, role of, 15-16
 gifts, 16-17, 25, 134
 librarian, role of, 15-16
 policy statement, 16-17, 133-134
 procedures, 17
 sources, 18
Books
 collation of, 103
 dusting of, 104
 effects of humidity on, 104-105
 handling of, 104
 insect damage, 105-106
 inspection of, 22, 103
 markings on exterior, 22, 59, 103
 markings on interior, 24, 46, 103
 mildew prevention, 104
 progress through preparation procedure, 47-60
 shelving of, 104
Borrower's identification, 13
Budget, 6-7, 22
Building, See Architecture and building
Call numbers, 43-46
 definition, 112
 location in book, 46
 location on exterior of book, 59
 method of printing on exterior of book, 59
 on catalog cards, 50
Card catalog
 codes of rules, 61
 description, 26, 61
 filing into. See Filing of catalog cards
 size, 61
Catalog cards
 added entry, 35, 53-54
 Bible main entry, 37-38
 collation, 27-28, 50-51, 94-97, 99
 compiler main entry, 36
 corporate main entry, 36, 50
 editor main entry, 36
 format, 50-54
 imprint, 27, 50
 main entry, 35-38, 47-52
 nonbook materials, 86, 87, 89, 94, 95, 96, 97, 100-101
 organization main entry, 36-37, 50
 personal author main entry, 27, 35, 50
 preparation of, 26-28, 31-32, 33-34, 47-50, 52-54, 86-89, 94, 95, 96, 97, 100-101
 preparation of sets, 52
 title added entry, 35, 54
 title main entry, 37

135

tracings, 32, 47-48, 51
typing of, 47-54
Cataloging of
  books, 26-38
  filmstrips, 96
  maps, 94
  microforms, 90
  motion picture films, 97
  periodicals, 85-87
  recordings, 99-100
  serials, 87-89
  slides, 95
  three-dimensional materials, 98
  transparencies, 97
  See also Descriptive cataloging,
    Subject cataloging
Charts, 95
Circulation card
  for nonbook materials, 81, 93, 96, 102
  information included, 11
  pocket for, 11
  preparation of, 56, 58
Circulation service, 11-14
  borrowers, type of, 13
  procedures, 11-12
  regulations, 13-14
  reserve book service, 12
  statistics, 12-13
  See also Circulation under specific
    types of materials: Filmstrips;
    Recordings, etc.
Classification, 39-46
  broad classification, 42
  close classification, 42
  definition of, 26, 39, 112
  principles and procedures, 42-46
  relation to subject headings, 42-43
Classification, Close. See Classification
Classification of
  biography, 45
  criticism, 45
  fiction, 46
  filmstrips, 96
  maps, 94
  microforms, 90
  monographic series, 89
  motion picture films, 97
  pamphlets, 80-81
  recordings, 99-100
  slides, 95
Classification systems, 39
  selection of, 39-40
  See also Dewey Decimal Classification
    system
Clippings, 79-80
Collation
  definition, 113
  in book examination, 22, 103
  in descriptive cataloging, 27-28, 50-51,
    94-97, 99

Compiler main entry. See Catalog cards
Corner pockets. See Book pockets
Corporate main entry. See Catalog cards
Cross references. See References
Cutter number, 38, 44-46, 113
Cutter-Sanborn tables, 44

Date slips, 58, 59
Descriptive cataloging
  definition, 26, 113
  imprint, 27
  information included, 26-28
  nonbook materials, 86-89, 90, 94-97,
    99-101
  personal author entry, 27
Dewey Decimal Classification system, 39,
  40-46
  divisions of, 40-41
  use of, 41-46
Dictionary catalog, 61, 113
Dioramas. See Three-dimensional materials
Divided catalog, 29, 61, 113-114

Editor main entry. See Catalog cards
Fiction, classification of, 46
Filing of catalog cards, 62-75
  abbreviations, 64-65
  acronyms, 64
  arrangement, 62-63
  articles, 62-63
  author entry, 68-70
  Bible entry, 71-75
  compound words, 66
  given names, 68
  hyphenated words, 65-66
  initials, 64
  names, 67-68
  numerals, 67
  prepositions, 62-63
  procedures, 60
  punctuation, 63-64
  reference cards, 71
  subject entry, 70-71
  title entry, 70
  varient spellings, 66
  word-by-word arrangement, 62
Films. See Motion picture films
Filmstrips
  cataloging, 96
  circulation, 96
  classification, 96
  handling of, 96
  storage, 96
Fines, 13-14
Flat pictures. See Pictures
Furniture. See Architecture and building

Gifts, 16-17, 25, 134
Graphs. See Charts

136

Humidity in library buildings, 104-105

Imprint, 27, 50, 114
Insects; damage to books from, 105-106
Instruction in library use, 8, 10-11

Jobbers and wholesalers, 20, 22, 82
Journals. See Periodicals

Labeling of books. See Books
Librarian
    administrator, 3-8
    book selection, role in, 15-16
Library, administration of. See
    Administration
Library instruction. See Instruction in
    library use
Library of Congress Classification system, 39
Library orientation. See Orientation

Magazines. See Periodicals
Main entries. See Catalog cards
Management, 3-5
    communication, 4
    delegation, 4
    objectives, 3
Maps
    cataloging, 94
    classification, 94
    storage, 94
Microfiche. See Microforms
Microfilm. See Microforms
Microforms
    cataloging, 90
    classification, 90
    equipment for reading, 90, 102
    purpose, 89
    storage, 90
Models. See Three-dimensional materials
Monographic series. See Series
Motion picture films
    cataloging, 97
    circulation, 97
    classification, 97
    equipment for, 102
Multi-media materials. See Nonbook materials; specific types: Motion picture films, Recordings, Slides, etc.

Nonbook materials, 76-102
    criteria for selection, 76-79
    definition, 76
    See also specific types: Periodicals, Recordings, Slides, etc.

Organization main entry. See Catalog cards
Orientation, 10-11

Pamphlets
    circulation, 81-82
    classification, 80-81
    description, 76, 115
    file maintenance, 76, 82
    processing, 80-81
    sources, 79
    storage, 81
Periodical indexes, 10, 82, 124-125
Periodicals
    binding, 85
    cataloging, 85-87
    checking in, 83
    definition, 115
    ordering, 82-83
    records of, 83, 84
    selection, 82-83
    storage, 83, 85
Personal author entry. See Catalog cards
Personnel, 4-6
    selection, 5
    training, 5
Phonodisc. See Recordings
Phonotape. See Recordings
Picture file. See Pictures
Pictures
    circulation, 93
    classification, 92-93
    filing, 93
    mounting, 91-92
    processing, 91-92
    purpose, 91
    selection, 91
    sources, 91
    storage, 91
    subject index, 93
Phonorecords. See Recordings
Postcards, 92
Posters. See Charts
Public relations, 8

Realia. See Three-dimensional materials
Recordings
    cataloging, 99-101
    circulation, 102
    classification, 99-101
    equipment for, 102
    processing, 99-100
    storage, 102
Recordings, disc. See Recordings
Recordings, tape. See Recordings
Reference books. 9-10, 119-125
Reference service, 7-8, 9-11
References, 30, 36-37, 51-52, 55, 71, 80-81
Reserve book service, 12

Selection. See Book selection; Selection under special types of materials: Filmstrips, Periodicals, Recordings, etc.
Serials
    cataloging, 87-89

definition, 82, 116
  See also Periodicals
Series, 32, 51, 54, 89, 116
Series analytic cards, 89
Shelf list, 24, 33-34, 43, 46, 53,
    87-88, 94, 95, 117
Shelf listing, 33-34
Slides
  cataloging, 95
  classification, 95
  equipment for, 102
Staff. See Personnel
Stamping of library materials, 22, 56,
    59, 83, 97, 102, 103
Statistics
  of books added to collection, 24
  of books prepared, 60
  of library loans, 12-13
Subject added entry. See Subject cataloging
Subject analytic cards, 30-31, 117
Subject catalog, 28-29, 61
Subject cataloging
  definition, 28-29
  nonbook materials, 80, 89, 92-93, 94,
    95, 96, 97, 101
  procedures, 30-32, 53
Subject heading list, 29
Subject headings, 29-30
  assignment of, 30-32
  for pictures, 92-93
  location of on card, 32, 47-48, 51
  relation to classification, 30
  specificity, 30-31

Three-dimensional materials
  cataloging, 98
  definition, 98
  dioramas, 98
  models, 98
  realia, 98
  storage, 98
Title added entry. See Catalog cards;
    Filing of catalog cards
Title main entry. See Catalog cards;
    Filing of catalog cards
Tracings, 32, 47-48, 51
  See also Subject headings
Transparencies
  cataloging, 97
  definition, 97
  equipment for, 102

Vertical file, 81, 93, 96, 100
  See also Pamphlets

Weeding, 82, 118
Work mark, 44, 46